More
Devon
Murders

John Van der Kiste

The History Press

First published 2011

The History Press
The Mill, Brimscombe Port
Stroud, Gloucestershire, GL5 2QG
www.thehistorypress.co.uk

British Library Cataloguing in Publication Data.
A catalogue record for this book is available from the British Library.

ISBN 978 0 7524 5956 1

Typesetting and origination by The History Press
Printed in Malta by Melita Press

CONTENTS

ALSO BY THE AUTHOR

A Divided Kingdom
A Grim Almanac of Cornwall
A Grim Almanac of Devon
A Grim Almanac of Hampshire
Berkshire Murders
Childhood at Court 1819–1914
Cornish Murders (with Nicola Sly)
Cornwall's Own
Crowns in a Changing World
Dearest Affie (with Bee Jordaan)
Dearest Vicky, Darling Fritz
Devon Murders
Edward VII's Children
Emperor Francis Joseph
Frederick III
George III's Children
George V's Children
Gilbert & Sullivan's Christmas
Kaiser Wilhelm II
King George II and Queen Caroline

Kings of the Hellenes
More Cornish Murders (with Nicola Sly)
More Somerset Murders (with Nicola Sly)
Northern Crowns
Once a Grand Duchess (with Coryne Hall)
Plymouth History & Guide
Princess Victoria Melita
Queen Victoria's Children
Somerset Murders (with Nicola Sly)
Sons, Servants and Statesmen
Surrey Murders
The Georgian Princesses
The Little Book of Devon
The Plymouth Book of Days
The Romanovs 1818-1959
West Country Murders (with Nicola Sly)
William and Mary
William John Wills
Windsor and Habsburg

AUTHOR'S NOTE & ACKNOWLEDGEMENTS

When my book *Devon Murders* was first published in 2006, my research had already covered a number of interesting cases which had to be shelved for lack of space. One thing leads to another, and writing on various other local history projects in the intervening years has led me on to the trail of several more. It was soon inevitable that there would be enough for a second volume at least.

As in *Devon Murders*, I have taken the opportunity of examining murders from town and country, from eras long since gone and from those still just within living memory. There are some which began, as they often do, as domestic differences between spouses or partners and escalated into tragedy, exacerbated by drunkenness, weak-mindedness or jealousy on one side. Others involve robbery with violence, or child abuse which went unchecked. From medieval times, I have also found a dispute involving officials from Exeter city and the cathedral, and a matter of dynastic rivalry between the two most powerful families of the area which culminated in bloodshed. Perhaps most remarkable of all is the mystery in which a young woman from a well-to-do Victorian family eloped with a suitor well-known for suspect business dealings, and was found drowned only a few days after her marriage.

There are several people to whom I am greatly indebted for help during the course of producing this book. Simon Dell MBE QCB has been a mine of information with regard to certain questions about police procedure and the Laura Dimes and Constable John Potter cases, in addition to allowing me the run of his personal collection of illustrations. Nicola Sly, with whom I have collaborated on similar titles in the past, generously allowed me the benefit of her research on the Frances Clarke case, as well as her own illustrations. Images have also been generously supplied by Steve Fielding, Derek Tait, Trevor James, and Paul Rendell, and Tony Lethbridge supplied additional information. Finally, my thanks as ever within the family go to my wife Kim for reading through the draft manuscript, to her and Russ Parkin for help with photography, and at The History Press to my commissioning editor, Matilda Richards.

John Van der Kiste
Devon, 2011

1

THE MURDERING MAYOR

Scandal, violence and even murder involving the Church were not unusual in medieval times. Nevertheless, even by thirteenth century standards, the events in Exeter were exceptional, and were only resolved by royal intervention.

In 1283 John Pycot, a well-known man of the area with a somewhat dubious reputation, was elected Dean of Exeter in rather suspicious circumstances. Bishop Peter Quinel questioned his election, refused to recognise him as Dean, and took

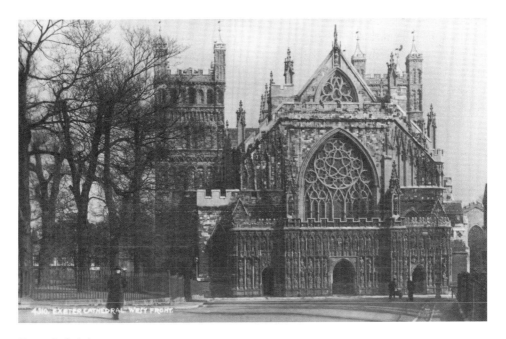

Exeter Cathedral.

steps to have him removed from office. There was some dissent in the chapter and controversy throughout the city, with many of the churchmen taking sides. It culminated in a sorry end for Walter Lechlade, one of Bishop Quinel's supporters. After attending matins and walking back across Cathedral Close in the early hours of 5 November 1283, he was hunted down by a gang of Pycot's men who had been lying in wait for him. They seized him, stabbed him to death and left his body on the spot. Lechlade's outraged family brought proceedings against Pycot, Alured de Porta, the mayor of Exeter, and nineteen other men whom they believed had blood on their hands.

As some of the supposedly great and good of the city were involved and doubtless had friends in high places in the judiciary, the legal formalities took much longer than anyone had expected. Weary of the endless delays, and concerned at what was being done to the good name of Exeter, two years later Bishop Quinel made a request to King Edward I, asking him to intercede and help to expedite a judgement in the case.

On 22 December King Edward, Queen Eleanor and three of their daughters arrived in Exeter, and on Christmas Eve he came to court and listened attentively to the facts of the case. Next morning, on Christmas Day, he and his family attended divine service. He then pronounced judgement on Porta and four of his henchmen, Elias Poyfed, Richard Stonyng, Thomas Amener, and Roger Twate, to hang for their part in the murder. They all went to the gallows on 26 December. Pycot's life was spared, but he was removed from his position and from public life altogether by being banished to a monastery.

Rarely if ever in British legal history can a city mayor have been hanged for murder, let alone during his period in office. His execution left Exeter without a mayor until David Cissor, sometimes called David Taylor, a tailor by profession – rather appropriately, in view of the name – was appointed to the vacant office.

At first, the Church authorities thought there might be repercussions from Pycot's friends and associates, and feared for their safety. A few days later the King granted permission to Quinel to enclose the Cathedral Yard with a wall 12ft high, and to allow the building of seven gates that would be kept closed overnight from dusk to dawn in order to keep people out.

Note: As might be expected with events so long ago, there are some discrepancies regarding dates. Some sources say that Pycot was elected in 1281, and that the murder took place on 10 not 5 November. Alured de Porta's name is sometimes given as Alfred or Alphred Duport.

2

THE MAD MONK
OF HALDON

Haldon Hill, 1329

For a time, fourteenth-century Devon harboured the man who has the dubious claim on posterity of being possibly England's first serial killer. During the daytime, Brother Robert de Middlecote was to all outward appearances a pious God-fearing monk at Lidwell Chapel, on the slopes of Haldon Hill near Exeter, where he heard the confessions of travellers who crossed the heath. By night he was a robber and a murderer.

The true facts about any character of the age are inevitably obscured in legend and by the constant embellishment of lurid stories from one generation to the next, and some of what is ostensibly known about the man may have little basis in fact. It is said that he had initially been a monk at the private Wallen Chapel, Gidleigh, where he was installed to say daily masses and look after the building. In March 1328 he attacked Agnes, the pregnant daughter of a local miller, and murdered her unborn child. Rumour had it that he had broken his vows of chastity, and that the child was his, or else that she was an unmarried girl who was carrying some other man's child, and he believed he had been ordered by God to carry out orders by killing an infant born out of wedlock. For his crime he was summoned for trial before the King's Justice, but he knew his rights and demanded to be tried by canon instead of secular law, meaning that he would probably receive a much lighter sentence from the ecclesiastical court.

The case was set for June 1328, but no records of subsequent proceedings were ever traced. It was thought that he might have convinced the court that his accusers were committing perjury, that he might have escaped custody and fled, or that the affair was hushed up and he was acquitted on condition that he agreed to leave the district and settle elsewhere. In view of subsequent history, the last outcome was the most likely. Because of the resulting scandal, the chapel was desecrated, left abandoned and used as a cattle shelter until it gradually became a ruin.

Within a few months, he was installed at Lidwell Chapel on Haldon Hill. This was situated at a remote spot north-west of Teignmouth, named after the nearby farm of Lidwell, or Lady's Well, after the holy well next to the chapel. It was thought that he would be out of harm's way here, and at first he apparently discharged his duties faithfully by day.

However when dusk fell, to take a modern analogy, Dr Jekyll became Mr Hyde, as he went in search of lonely travellers who were exhausted, hungry and eager to take up his offers of shelter, food, drink and rest. The chapel was well illuminated and easily visible to those who were journeying from Teignmouth, the busiest port on the nearby coast. Once they had entered the building, the unsuspecting visitor was supplied with a hot meal, to which poison had been added. As soon as he was semi-conscious, Brother Robert stabbed him to death, stripped the body of any valuables, and dropped it down the well behind the chapel door.

The remains of Lidwell Chapel. (© Kim Van der Kiste)

Inevitably, success soon went to his head. One sailor, more fortunate than most, was praying in the chapel when his host tried to catch him unawares, but the quick-witted man overpowered him and pushed him down the well. There are two versions of what happened next. According to one, the monk, having learned his lesson, was hauled up half-drowned, and died a few minutes later. The other suggests that the sailor obtained help from the nearby farm, and his assailant was arrested, none the worse for his ordeal. He was taken to Exeter, and found guilty of assault. All the evidence was purely circumstantial, as there was nobody to prove that he had killed other people, despite his fearsome reputation in the neighbourhood, but it did not save him from being hanged from the city gallows as a multiple murderer.

A reference in the *Bishop's Register* of May 1329 refers to 'the purgation of Robert de Middlecote'. To posterity, he is known as 'the mad monk of Haldon'. There is a theory that the isolation drove him mad, although he was more probably a greedy opportunist who felt he could commit crime after crime and get away with it – until he chanced his luck on one occasion too many.

Only a single wall and foundations of Lidwell Chapel, situated in a field some distance from the road, still remain. Grass and trees have long since been growing wild around the shell, and it is plentifully strewn with weeds. Some visitors are convinced that the area lies under a curse, and that it radiates an aura of evil.

It might be noted that the Haldon Hill area has featured prominently in two other murder cases, both during the twentieth century. In February 1947 the body of teenager Doreen Messenger (*see* chapter 27) was found there. Over thirty years later, in September 1983, the headless body of a young woman in cycling shorts and T-shirt was also discovered in the area. She was identified as Monika Zumsteg-Telling, the missing wife of Michael Telling. The couple's unhappy marriage had been marked by increasingly bitter quarrels until he killed her at their home in Buckinghamshire, drove to Devon and left her decapitated body there, keeping the head at home in an effort to avoid identification. The following year he was found guilty of manslaughter on the grounds of diminished responsibility and imprisoned for life.

During the late twentieth century a photographer took some shots of the Lidwell Chapel ruins, and was astonished when the results showed the chapel intact, as it would have been at the time those unwary travellers were lured to their doom. A few years later, another photographer tried to take several pictures of the chapel as well, but none of them came out. More recently, members of the present author's family did likewise. At home that evening, the images just taken could be seen intact on the digital camera, but next day they had gone – and in the process, a large number of pictures taken on the same camera on several previous occasions had also been mysteriously wiped. As the illustration opposite shows, a subsequent attempt about six months later proved more successful.

3

A FATAL FAMILY FEUD

Near Exeter, 1455

The dynastic conflicts and series of resulting battles fought between 1455 and 1485, known to posterity as the Wars of the Roses, were reflected in the changing fortunes of many of the great aristocratic families of the age. Although they did not necessarily play any part in the struggle for the throne between the houses of Lancaster and York, some of the local feuds could lead to bitterness, and in one instance even murder.

Nicholas Radford, a respected Devonshire attorney, was apparently liked by leading members of the two main noble families of the area, the Bonvilles and the Courtenays. He was a councillor of Lord Bonville, but at the same time he worked for many years with the Courtenays, the Earls of Devon. In 1423 he was appointed surveyor and steward of the lands of Thomas Courtenay, fifth Earl of Devon, who was a minor at the time. The men evidently became close family friends, and in around 1440 Radford was asked to stand as godfather to the Earl's baby son Henry. Later he served as a trustee with Devon for the lands of several other members of the Courtenay family.

Nevertheless, his friendship with the Bonvilles was about to cause difficulties for him. It is thought that he may have represented one or more of the family in a successful lawsuit against the Courtenays, something the latter would not readily forgive or forget. At the very least, he had become a close friend of Lord Bonville, whose family was seen as probably the most important in the area after the Courtenays.

All that is known for certain is that a feud between them had been gathering apace for some time, and was about to claim an unwitting victim. The Earl and his sons launched a series of raids and attacks on the properties and supporters of the Bonville family, and Radford was viewed as one of their legitimate targets. At around midnight on 23 October 1455, Thomas Courtenay, the Earl's heir, led an armed mob, probably about a hundred strong, to Radford's country estate, Upcott Barton, about eleven miles north of Exeter. According to one source they did a certain amount of damage, including setting fire to the main gates, before making their way to directly outside the house. Here they created a disturbance which awoke everyone, and ordered Radford to come outside and talk to them.

Although he knew the men were led by the Courtenays, the unsuspecting Radford did not think he would come to any harm, and made his way towards them. As he did so the men broke into the house, taking any money and possessions they could lay hands on. They showed no mercy to his invalid wife Thomasina, throwing her from her bed on to the floor as she shook with terror, and removing the sheets as part of their haul.

Meanwhile Courtenay demanded that Radford accompany him to meet his father at Tiverton, about six miles away, on urgent business. Hopelessly outnumbered, Radford had no choice but to agree. Only then did he discover to his dismay that the men had taken his horses, so he would have to walk the whole distance. Once they were a short way from the house, Courtenay left him. This was the cue for six of his men to set upon Radford, stabbing him, cutting his throat and leaving him dying on the road from his wounds.

About four days later, Radford's body was being prepared for burial at Upcott chapel. A party led by Henry Courtenay, the murdered man's godson and the Earl's second son, forced their way in and held a mock inquest, declaring that he had committed suicide and could not be given a Christian burial. Courtenay then ordered his men to seize the body and take it to the churchyard at Cheriton Fitzpaine, where they threw it into a grave and pelted it with stones Radford had purchased to place on his grave after burial until it was unrecognisable, thus not fit for a proper inquest.

In November, the Earl and his two sons placed themselves at the head of an armed force of 1,000 men. Marching from Tiverton to Exeter, they seized the gates of the city, set their own watch, and remained there for the next six weeks. During that time, the Earl compelled the Dean and Treasurer of the cathedral to surrender to them goods to the value of £600, and £700 in money, with which Radford had entrusted them for safekeeping. A couple of days later, about a hundred of the Earl's followers raided a house in Exeter which had belonged to Radford, taking away more money and a large collection of valuable plate and jewels. They may have needed the goods as plunder to pay and divide up among the mercenaries responsible for doing their dirty work, or robbery might have been a motive for the murder.

The Earl of Devon may or may not have authorised his men to kill Radford, but whoever was responsible, it was clearly a case of premeditated murder. He had everything to gain from it, and played his part in shielding the guilty man or men from justice. Nobody was ever held to account for the unfortunate lawyer's violent death. Yet even in an age where savagery was a way of life, the episode and its aftermath shocked contemporaries and did much to blacken the Courtenays' name for a generation. The family were leading adherents of the Lancastrian cause in the West Country, and their behaviour was thought to have been partly down to the inept rule of the pious but weak-minded King Henry VI and his advisers.

In London there were calls by members of parliament for the more capable Richard, Duke of York, to be appointed Protector of the Realm a second time. He had previously held this office for a while during a period between 1453 and 1454, when the King had been mentally ill and incapable of discharging his kingly duties. York was duly reappointed, but the Courtenays had friends in high places. Despite the protests of John Radford, the heir and cousin of the murdered man, the Courtenays and the three men who were suspected of wielding the fatal blows were granted royal pardons.

Justice of a kind was seen to be done some five years later. Thomas Courtenay, sixth Earl of Devon, who had almost certainly instigated the murder, was among those fighting under the Lancastrian banner at the battle of Towton, Yorkshire in 1461, a few weeks after King Henry VI had been deposed and the son of the recently slain Duke of York had been declared King Edward IV. Towton was a heavy defeat for the Lancastrians, with more people believed to have been killed in this battle on British soil before or since. The Earl was among those members of the nobility on the losing side who was captured and beheaded afterwards. A correspondent of John Paston noted tersely that, 'The Earl of Devonshire is dead justly.'

4

'JUDGE AND REVENGE MY CAUSE, O GOD'

Plymouth, 1672

In August 1672, Mrs Weeks of Plymouth, the wife of William Weeks, a dyer, was taken ill with severe gastric trouble. Her symptoms included acute internal pain, cold sweats, fainting, and severe vomiting, and a few days later she died in agony. Shortly afterwards William and their daughter, and granddaughter, suffered from a similar illness. The physician who attended them suspected they had been deliberately poisoned. When a neighbour visited the family and noticed a pot in the kitchen containing arsenic, his suspicions were as good as confirmed.

At around the same time the nurse, Philippa Cary and a servant girl, Anne Evans, also became unwell. In their case the symptoms were less severe, and they recovered after being given emetics. The child and Mr Weeks recovered, but his daughter died.

Tongues soon began to wag. Cary and Evans were both arrested on suspicion of murder, and were brought for questioning separately before the mayor. Anne Evans, who was only aged 13, and had been placed in service by the churchwardens and overseers of Charles Parish after her mother died, said that she had bought 'a pottle of girts' in the market. After she had cooked it, she noticed that an odd-looking yellow substance had formed, but it did not smell unusual. She served it to the family, and they became ill immediately afterwards.

It soon became clear that neither servant liked each other much, and regardless of who was telling the truth (if either of them was), each was determined to save her own skin and incriminate the other. When Cary was asked, she said that she had had an argument with Mrs Weeks, about frying pilchards. Cary had asked Evans afterwards if she knew where she could buy any rat poison. Lest it be thought that she wanted it in order to do away with their mistress, she also said that Anne Evans was on very bad terms with Mrs Weeks, and had threatened to run away and join 'the mountebanks'.

When spoken to a second time, Anne Evans said that while she was gathering herbs, she found a packet of poison. As she showed it to Cary, the latter told her that it was just the very thing needed to 'fit' Mrs Weeks, and only a small dose was required to 'make work.' She also said that Cary had scolded her for removing a large spider from a glass of beer as Mrs Weeks was just about to drink it. At that time, it was widely believed that spiders were poisonous. 'Thou shouldst have let it alone, thou fool,' Cary had told her, 'and not have taken it out, but shouldst have squatted it amongst the beer.'

Reminded later of having said this, Cary indignantly denied it, saying instead that Evans had made threats to 'do away' with her mistress. Next, Evans said she saw Cary crushing the rat's bane into fine powder between two tiles, and when she asked what she was doing, replied that she was making a medicine to 'fit' Mrs Weeks, to whom she now referred to contemptuously as 'the old woman'. After putting the powder in a dish, she added some beer, and allowed the mixture to stand overnight. She then gave Anne some of the poison to add to Mrs Weeks's porridge next morning, with the ominous words, 'You shall see what sport we shall have with her to-morrow.'

The amount they gave her was very small, and only caused her mild discomfort. Cary then told her, 'We shall live so merry as the days are long,' adding that as long as Anne held her tongue, they would be safe; but if she was to breathe a word to anybody else and 'betray' them, she would have to take all the blame.

When Mrs Weeks asked for her porridge, Anne added the arsenic into the bowl according to Cary's instructions. Mrs Weeks ate all of hers, and later Cary offered some to Mr Weeks, but he did not like the taste and passed it on to the rest of the family to try. They all said it tasted odd, and though they only sampled a small amount, they all had convulsions. Alarmed to see the family in such agony, Anne asked Cary later what she had been doing, 'that our master and mistress are so very ill?'

When an inquiry was made into the case, according to a statement from Anne, Cary replied that, 'she had done God good service in it to rid her out of the way, and that she had done no sin in it.' This confession was read to Cary, who denied having made any such remark.

Cary and Evans were both held in custody, to await the next Exeter assizes. They found themselves 'in the very suburbs of Hell,' for the local prison was no better than 'a seminary of all villainies, prophaneness and impieties.' When they came to court before Lord Chief Justice North, according to observers they replied to the questions put to them 'with heavy hearts though with undejected countenances.'

They were found guilty of murder and sentenced to death, and a plea to the judge that they should be transported instead was refused. The judge ordered that Anne Evans was 'to be drawn on a hurdle to the place where she shall be executed, and there burnt to death.' One of those in court, John Quicke, a Nonconformist minister, later wrote a pamphlet in which he said that 'the very sentence should have struck her dead; an emblem and lively picture of Hell's torments. Drawn as if dragged by devils. Burnt alive, as if in the Lake of Fire and Brimstone already.' Philippa Cary was ordered to hang till she was dead. 'Too gentle a death, for such a prodigy of ungodliness,' wrote Quicke. 'She pleads stiffly her innocence, disowns her guilt, takes no shame, her brow is brass, she is impudent and hath a whore's forehead. If ever there were a daughter of Hell, this is one in her proper colours. No evidence shall convince her.'

'Confess,' she told Evans, 'then I shall hang indeed. I deny the fact, none saw, none knew it but the girl; it may be that vile person, my husband, hath a hand in it, but he is gone. Some will pity me, though none will believe me, none can help me.' Now, according to Quicke, Satan helped Cary to 'an expedient that may help her life.' She pleaded before the judge that she was expecting a child, asking that if she must die, at least let her child live. The judge ordered a jury of matrons to be empanelled, but when they examined her they found she was lying.

As Plymouth had been the scene of the murder, the judge agreed to a petition from Mrs Weeks's family that the execution should be carried out there, on condition that the town magistrates, or Mr Weeks himself, would meet the expenses, and as long as they could arrange for it to occur in good time, otherwise the gallows would be erected at Exeter. 'The day of execution is to be on Thursday in Easter week, but if you, the magistrate of the said town, or Mr Weeks, shall fail to undertake before Easter Day to defray the extraordinary charges thereof, then the execution on these malefactors is to be done at the common-place of execution for this County.'

The local authorities accordingly made suitable arrangements. In the seventeenth century, public executions were then regarded by many as an exciting spectacle not to be missed. There was also a moral purpose, in that the authorities hoped that the punishments would act as 'a moral warning' to others.

Cary was encouraged to confess by church ministers that she had been responsible, but she continued to insist that Anne Evans was the guilty party. John Quicke warned her that:

> she had sworn a bargain with the Devil for secrecy to her own destruction, that all would come out at last, as cunningly and closely as she did carry it before men and angels; and, said I, you are one of the most bloody women that ever came into gaol; you are guilty of two murders, one of your master, another of your mistress, and a third of having drawn in this poor girl like a Devil, as you are, to joyn with you to ruin them and herself also.

He further assured her that he did 'as verily believe she would be in Hell, unless there were a very wonderful change wrought upon her, as that old Murderer, her Father, the Devil, was.' His efforts to persuade her proved unsuccessful. When Cary implored him to have some pity and indulgence towards her, he refused to do so till he knew that 'her stony heart was riven and shivered in pieces and her bones broken under her hellish wickedness.'

Waiting outside the cell door whilst this denunciation was being delivered was 'a crowd of vulgar persons,' all keen to obtain admission. The gaolers profited handsomely by charging the inquisitive and curious a few pence for admission to see criminals condemned to death, and they reaped a good harvest on this occasion.

As the time for their executions drew nearer, Quicke assured the condemned woman and girl that it was quite as 'easy going to Heaven from the stake and the gallows as if it was from their beds,' but they must still confess their guilt. Cary still refused to do so. Quicke lost patience with her, and he abused her roundly as 'a brazen impudent hypocrite thus to dissemble with God and man', warning her that, as she kept the devil's counsel, to the devil she would go, and that he saw no promise of a good result if he expended any more labour upon her. 'Look to it, woman,' he delivered as a parting shot, 'that this do not make thy Hell hotter than ordinary.'

While the prisoners were led from Exeter on horseback, Cary exchanged 'ribald and obscene jests' with the spectators, and as they drew near Plymouth the procession was met by thousands eager to catch sight of the condemned party. Not surprisingly, there was an air of general sympathy for Evans, but none for the elder servant who had shamelessly led her astray and then tried to hold her fully responsible. Several ministers came to talk to them as they were taken to their cells prior to execution, but inquisitive crowds continued to push their way forward, tipping the gaolers in order to catch sight of the criminals. Cary remained resolute in denying her guilt, but Evans confessed hers.

On the appointed day they were escorted to the gallows erected on the heights of Prince Rock. Quicke described the occasion:

> The streets were crowded, the Mayor, the Magistrates and Under Sheriff can hardly pass for the throng. The poor maid was drawn on the hurdle. The posture she lay in was on her left side, her face in her bosom, her Bible under her arm, seeming like one dead rather than alive. At length we came, though slowly, to the place of execution. Plymouth was then naked of inhabitants, the town was easy to be taken, and the houses to be plundered, if an enemy had been at hand to have done it. Cattedown, the Lambhay, the Citadel, and Cattewater are pressed with a multitude of twenty thousand persons. But commanders, who have lived in wars and seen great armies, and are therefore the most competent judges in this case, estimate them at one-half. I write within compass. The maid, being nailed to the stake, and the iron hoop about her, and the nurse mounted on the ladder, she desires that the Relater may pray with her.

The crowds were invited to join in the singing of a psalm, during which, Quicke noted, 'the clear childish voice' of Anne Evans was heard 'to rise like that of the lark'. Afterwards he read several long prayers, as a rope was drawn tightly round her neck:

> The hangman would have set fire unto the furze before she was strangled; but some, more charitable and tender-hearted, cried to him to take away the block from under her feet, which having been done, she soon fell down and expired in a trice.

It took the executioner quarter of an hour after she was dead to get the powder, wood and fuel to catch fire. As the flames rose higher, the wind blew the smoke into the face of the nurse, 'as if God had spoken to her; the smoke of My Fury and Flames of My Fiery Vengeance are now riding upon the wings of the wind towards thee.'

For two hours Cary had to stay and watch her reluctant accomplice burn, and further efforts were made to wring a confession from her, but in vain. When the time came for her to die, the executioner was missing. He was found drunkenly lying under the cliffs, holding the halter, and the search party carried him to the foot of the gallows, to sleep off his over-indulgence. Further futile efforts were made by the Nonconforming ministers to persuade her to repent and confess, while another hangman was sought to finish the job.

Her last words before being swung into the air were, 'Judge and revenge my cause, O God.' To Quicke, it was 'a sure proof that she went into the lake of brimstone and fire, there to be tormented for ever and ever.'

Note: No date can be traced for the trial, but it probably took place at the Exeter winter assizes in late 1672.

5

THE DISAPPEARING VICAR OF HARTLAND

Hartland, 1811

In the eighteenth century, John Vine of Hartland and his wife were hard-working people, regular churchgoers, and well respected in the district. Their son, Peter, was born in 1776, and when he told them that he wanted to make his career within the Church they were delighted. After being provided with a good education, he took holy orders and was appointed vicar of Hartland. He worked diligently at preaching the gospel to the local community, made home visits to several of his parishioners on a regular basis, and undertook to teach some of the children whose parents could not afford to give them an education by any other means.

Everybody who came into contact with Peter liked him, but while he remained a bachelor, any friendships he made were bound to lead to gossip. Early in 1811, there were rumours that his frequent visits to the wealthy Mrs Dark might have some ulterior motive, especially as there was no mention of a Mr Dark (she was probably a widow) and she was a well-provided-for woman. The Revd Peter Vine taught her 11-year-old daughter, but neighbours wondered if there was any further reason for his regular presence at the house.

One day in January 1811 Vine went to Mrs Dark's house, as he had done so often before in order to give the girl her lessons. When he arrived, mother, daughter and vicar took a stroll through the garden together. After a while Mrs Dark left them and returned indoors. Almost as soon as she had gone, he proceeded to undo several years of good work in a single stroke. He seized the terrified child and raped her, then took to his heels, jumping over the garden wall, and running away from the village.

Mrs Dark was unaware that anything was going on until she heard screaming. When she returned to the garden, she was so horrified to find her violated daughter lying on the ground that she collapsed. At length a servant came out to find her, and discovered her still unconscious beside the young girl. Realising what

Hartland Point.

had happened, the servant raised the alarm. A thorough search of the villages was carried out, but Vine had made good his escape. When she had recovered her wits, Mrs Dark offered a reward of 20 guineas to anybody who could bring him to justice.

The community was shocked to the core that their hitherto respected vicar should have apparently let them down so badly. His parents, who still lived at Hartland, were particularly upset. Their home was searched on a regular basis, as the authorities were sure he must be hiding there, but they never found any sign of him. At the same time there were unconfirmed reports that he was laying low in Barnstaple or Bideford, or in the adjoining area. The neighbouring towns were scoured, but for three months there was no sign of him anywhere.

On Sunday 17 April, Vine returned casually to Hartland, as if nothing was wrong. Yet he was aware of the bounty on his head, and he told several people that he would not hesitate to shoot the first man who tried to apprehend him. When she was told that he had come back, Mrs Dark visited Mr Justice Saltern and obtained from him a warrant for his arrest, which she then took to the home of the Hartland constable. He had been advised of Vine's reappearance, and had two men at the ready for such an eventuality. The men, Roger Ashton and William Blake, were prepared to seek him and bring him back to the authorities.

Once the search was on, nobody had any intention of allowing the criminal in their midst any shelter. Ashton and Blake's enquiries soon led them to the house in which Vine was hiding. As he had barred all the doors and windows in anticipation of their arrival, they had to force their way in. Ashton was the first to enter the house, but Vine confronted him with a pistol at the ready, fired at point-blank range and Ashton was killed instantly. Vine was about to reload his weapon when Blake and the constable seized him, disarmed him and led him under arrest to Mr Justice Saltern.

When he was questioned, Vine denied having anything to do with the assault on Miss Dark, and his plea that he had killed Ashton in self-defence while resisting arrest did him no good. The elderly John Vine, who had been heartbroken by the news of what had happened to Miss Dark, made his way to Saltern's house and had an emotional interview with his son, telling him: 'you in whom lay all my delight and pleasure of this life, now proves the destroyer of it!' Afterwards he took to his bed and died ten days later.

Vine was put on trial at the Guildhall, Exeter, on 25 April 1811, where the jury found him guilty of the rape of a child and of the wilful murder of Roger Ashton. He continued to deny the former charge but freely admitted to the latter. As there had been two witnesses to the deed, he could hardly have done otherwise, and a sentence of death was passed. While in his cell awaiting execution – scheduled for 4 May – he spoke to the other prisoners, with whom he prayed regularly.

When the final day arrived and he took the short walk from the cell to the gallows, he turned and made a speech to the crowds, who had assembled to see justice done. He remained adamant that he was guilty of only one of the crimes ascribed to him, claiming that in shooting Mr Ashton he was merely defending himself, as Ashton had never told him his business when he came to arrest him, and he only fired the pistol because he feared for his life and thought he was going to be robbed. As for his absconding from the town, he said that it was because he had received news of the illness of his father. It was a dignified address, but failed to convince anyone present. Nobody could find any motive for his crimes apart from sheer wickedness, and he died unlamented by all.

Note: Some sources give the year of Vine's crimes and execution as 1743.

6

'A LARGE QUANTITY OF OIL OF VITRIOL'

Buckfastleigh, 1817

In 1817 Frances Clarke, also known as Frances Puttavin, a single woman thought to be in her early thirties, went before the parish at Buckfastleigh. Homeless and heavily pregnant, she was placed in lodgings with William Vesey, a labourer, and his wife Susannah. Early in October, she gave birth to a healthy baby boy, whom she named after the man she called his father, George Lakeman, a local farmer.

On the morning of 24 October, she was sitting by the fire with the infant asleep in her lap. Shortly after midday, Susannah Vesey suggested that she should put the baby to rest upstairs. Frances agreed, took him upstairs and laid him on the bed, then came down, going back to the baby almost at once with an apron over her arm. A minute or two afterwards, William Vesey heard choking sounds from the room upstairs, and called to ask Frances what was going on. To his horror, she told him quite calmly that the baby was dying. She then picked him up in her arms and came back downstairs with him, where she met Susannah.

To Susannah's astonishment, George was now coughing and struggling to breathe. Susannah asked Frances to let her take him but the mother refused, clutching the baby tightly and rushing upstairs again with him. Suspicious that something strange was going on, Susannah followed as Frances made it plain she was trying to avoid her, still clinging desperately to the baby. At length Susannah caught up with her, wrested baby George, now screaming, from her grasp, and took him over to the window to look at him properly in the light. His mouth was open, and she saw something inside which looked as if it was boiling. She could also see what appeared to be a bloodstain on the baby's clothes, and as she touched it with her finger and placed it in her mouth, her tongue burned. She told Frances angrily that she had murdered her baby, but Frances did not react and made no effort to deny the charge.

Buckfastleigh, c. 1909. (© Nicola Sly)

Susannah sent for Nicholas Churchill, a local surgeon, saying she was sure a small child had been poisoned. When Churchill arrived, he found George blue in the face, his lips, mouth and tongue looking as if he had just swallowed some acid as he struggled pitifully to breathe. As he could do nothing he called another surgeon, Thomas Rowe, who did what he could but to no avail. The baby lingered on in agony for nearly twenty-four hours before dying at around midday on 25 October.

At an inquest at Buckfastleigh Town Hall on 26 October before coroner Joseph Gribble, the cause of the baby's death was given as poisoning by oil of vitriol. A verdict of wilful murder was returned against Frances Clarke, and she was committed to the county gaol at Exeter to stand trial before Mr Justice Holroyd at the next county assizes.

Frances stood trial for murder in early 1818. The principal witnesses for the prosecution were William and Susannah Vesey, and their maid, 11-year-old Sarah Maddock. Despite her tender years, the latter proved a truthful and coherent witness as she told the court that during the autumn of 1817, about six weeks before baby George died, Frances had sent her to Richard Butcher's shop in Buckfastleigh to buy a penny's worth of oil of vitriol, under orders to say that it was required for the Veseys if any questions should be asked. Sarah accordingly bought and paid for the oil of vitriol, with Butcher warning that if anyone drank the liquid, it would prove fatal. Sarah declared under oath that when she handed it over to Frances Clarke, she had repeated this information. Butcher then took the witness stand to confirm the purchase from his shop, although he said that the girl had told him she was shopping for Miss Clarke.

Churchill and Mr Rowe, the surgeons, thought the child had died after being given oil of vitriol (sulphuric acid). They had identified a small bluish mark on the side of the baby's nose, which Churchill suggested was characteristic of the application of sulphuric acid to skin. In order to demonstrate this, he produced a small phial of the substance, applied a little to his own finger, and compared the result with that which had been left on the child's nose. Other acids, he said, generally left yellow or white burn marks or stains on their sin, but only sulphuric acid a blue one, as it had done on his finger and on the baby's nose.

Next, two empty bottles found in the house after Frances Clarke's arrest were produced, one retrieved from a box in her possession and the other thrown on the fire. Either might have contained the poison from which the baby died. Sarah Maddock and Richard Butcher both testified that they were similar to that purchased on behalf of the prisoner, though they could not be certain that they were the same bottles. When asked for his opinion William Hallett, a chemist, said he was not sure what the bottles had contained. If they had been used to store oil of vitriol, and not been washed afterwards, they would still retain the pungent smell of acid, which would corrode anything with which it came into contact. Even if the bottle had been burned in a fire, it would have had no effect on any residue of its contents.

After Mr Justice Holroyd had summed up, the jury were invited to retire and consider their verdict. They said it was unnecessary to do so, and intended to pronounce her guilty of wilful murder. At this stage, the judge told the court that Miss Clarke had been charged with murdering her son, George Lakeman Clarke. As it had just come to light that he had officially been christened just George Lakeman,

it was possible that the entire trial might be invalid. Although he had thought fit to proceed in order to establish the defendant's guilt or innocence, he now found himself unable to pass sentence, and proposed to forward the case to the legal authorities for further consideration.

At her retrial, which probably took place in March 1819, Miss Clarke was charged with killing her baby through administering oil of vitriol, which had passed into his stomach. Similar evidence to that offered at the first trial was heard, and the medical witnesses stated that the fatal substance had not reached the child's stomach. Death had been due to damage to the throat and subsequent suffocation. For a second time she was acquitted on a technicality, or on faulty wording of the indictments.

On 6 August 1819, Frances was summoned to appear at Exeter Assizes, to be charged yet again before Mr Justice Best with the wilful

Exeter Guildhall, where the assizes were held.

murder of her son, George Lakeman, 'by compelling the infant to take a large quantity of oil of vitriol, by means whereof he became disordered in his mouth and throat and by the disorder choking, suffocating and strangling occasioned thereby, died on the following day.' The indictment added that he had 'died of a certain acid called oil of vitriol administered by the prisoner and taken into his mouth and throat whereby he became incapable of swallowing his food and that his death was the consequence of the inflammation, injury and disorder occasioned thereby.'

On being asked how she would plead, Frances evoked her former acquittal. This was overruled by Mr Justice Best, who told the court that the defendant must plead either 'Guilty' or 'Not Guilty'. If she pleaded not guilty 'she may have a writ of error to the Court of the King's Bench', the supreme court in England, or else he would submit the case for the opinion of twelve judges. In effect this meant that regardless of the court's findings, the prisoner would have the right of appeal. She pleaded 'Not Guilty' and the prosecution, led by Mr Selwyn, opened the case by calling William Vesey as a witness.

This time, Mr Tonkin and Mr Merewether were in court for the defence. As in the original trial, the court heard evidence from the Veseys and Sarah Maddock, and this time the Veseys' married daughter, Sarah Tupper, was called to testify. At the time of the death of baby George, Sarah Tupper had a young baby of her own and on the morning of the alleged murder, the mothers had sat together breastfeeding their respective infants.

Unlike George, Sarah Tupper's child had been sickly, and she had been very concerned for its health. Frances had assured her that she did not believe her own baby would live for long. They had discussed the fact that Frances had a 'nice bosom of milk to go wet nursing' but Frances said that if her baby should die she would allow her milk to dry up and move away from the area, somewhere in the countryside. Sarah Tupper then had to leave to go to work, and on returning to her parents' house shortly after midday, she found Frances sitting in the same place, her child still not dressed. Frances explained that little George had been asleep all morning and she was reluctant to disturb him.

Sarah had also been present when Frances was clasping the baby in her arms as he screamed in agony, and she had seen the damage to his mouth and throat, watching the liquid run from his mouth and burn his clothes. She said that she and Frances had both attempted to breastfeed him but he was unable to suckle, and commented that Frances seemed totally unperturbed by his distress. When cross-examined by the counsel for the defence, she was asked about the medicine bottle which was subsequently found in the prisoner's box, and she stated that it was not in Miss Clarke's possession, but was an 'open box', into which any member of the family might put things.

Richard Butcher was called again to confirm his statement regarding the sale from his shop of oil of vitriol to Sarah Maddock, and his verbal warning that the amount purchased would prove fatal. The surgeons told the court that acid had been administered to the child and that his symptoms were consistent with drinking oil of vitriol, which had caused inflammation and swelling of the throat and prevented him from breathing. They had not conducted a post-mortem examination.

Finally, Frances Clarke submitted a written statement denying her guilt. She insisted that she had previously raised other children 'tenderly', and spoke of three former masters who had given her a good character reference at her previous trial. During the proceedings, she fainted several times and had to be revived by prison warders so that the trial could continue.

In his summing up, Mr Justice Best told the jury that it was for them to decide if the child had died as a result of an act by the prisoner. He then reiterated the evidence presented so far, pointing out that even things which might appear insignificant acquired weight when considered cumulatively. After a few minutes the jury returned a verdict of 'Guilty', and Frances Clarke was sentenced to death for the wilful murder of her son, but the counsel for the defence raised an objection to the indictment. Mr Justice Best then agreed to forward the case for appeal.

However this proved unnecessary. No appeal was lodged, and though the thrice-tried Frances Clarke was almost certainly guilty of murder, she never went to the gallows. Twice she had been saved by badly-worded indictments, and on the third occasion royal intervention came to her rescue. The death of King George III on 29 January 1820 brought his eldest son and heir to the throne as George IV, and one of his first acts was to issue a statement marked for the attention of the judges on the western circuit. Having considered a report on the case, he was 'graciously pleased to Extend Our Grace and Mercy unto her and to Grant her Our Free Pardon for her said Crime'.

7

'THE DEVIL WILL DRAG THEM INTO HELL'

Okehampton, 1818

By 1818, Charles and Mary Woodman had been married for about ten years. For the last two of these Mary, whose age was given variously as thirty and thirty-eight and who was several years Charles' senior, had spent little time with him at their Okehampton home. Instead she had taken up with Richard Smallacombe, known as 'Smiler', a wandering fiddler who earned a precarious living by playing at country fairs, and was also involved in counterfeiting money. They travelled around the country together, living together almost as husband and wife, much to the distress of the ever-forgiving Charles Woodman, who longed to have Mary back.

When the fairs were finished for the season in October 1818, she returned to Devon. Charles heard that she was back, and he sent a friend to tell her that he wanted to see her again. When she came home he pleaded with her to stay, and seemed almost pathetically glad to have her home. However she was constantly rude to him, and did her best to make his life a misery. One day she asked him if he was in a position to maintain her. He told her resignedly that he could if he starved himself. She then told him that she was prepared to stay, as 'I shall be happy, you will be gone, and I shall have Smallacombe.'

Charles and their friends saw nothing more of Smiler, and they assumed that he had gone away to leave the couple in peace. They were unaware that he had gone no further than Exeter, where he was arrested and imprisoned for passing forged coins.

Nevertheless, Mary was sure that he was waiting for her. It was not part of Mary's plan that Charles should remain alive for long, and there was one easy way to hasten his demise. In December, she sent her sister, Agnes Pedlar, to go to Mr Lacey, the chemist, to buy some cream of tartar, saying she needed it to put on a blemish on her arm. Agnes apparently went and asked for arsenic 'by mistake', and when he refused to supply her with any, she went to Mr Brookes's chemist shop where, again, she asked for the poison in error. A little more trusting than the last, Mr Brookes sold her some, and she went to meet her sister in the market place. Mary sampled a small amount of the mixture very carefully, then spat it out and told her sister angrily that she must have bought the wrong substance. Agnes claimed she had carried out the errand for her sister, as her sister owed the chemist money and he would not sell her anything else until she had discharged her debts.

Mary and Charles had been invited to a wedding feast at Zeal, and while they were there mutual acquaintances commented on how happy they looked together. Mary played the part of the adoring wife to perfection. It provided her with the perfect cover for slipping poison into his drink. After they returned home Charles was violently sick, and took to his bed for two days. She had underestimated the dose needed to take fatal effect. The doctor was called, and told her that although her husband was in agony, as long as he was nursed carefully, he would be restored to health.

Their 9-year-old daughter, Mary Ann, had been sent by her mother to buy some litharge of gold a few days earlier, and when she returned home she saw her mother put it carefully in a small pot. Charles's mother, also Mary Woodman, was living with them at the time, and during a conversation, her daughter-in-law had said casually that Charles had become ill after drinking a pint of cider.

As he lay ill she went into town, and enrolled him in two 'sick clubs', insurance schemes which would pay out a small sum of money, about £20, in the event of his death. Next she went to purchase some arsenic, and administered it to him in some food on her return home.

On 12 December, Mary put arsenic on two pieces of bread and butter. Charles complained bitterly that he was burning to death. He died the next day, and was buried in Okehampton churchyard later that week. Far from expressing any

Zeal.

sorrow, Mary remarked nonchalantly that she would have to buy some mourning clothes, and then pay off all her debts.

The doctor who had been called to see Charles while he was ill had immediately suspected from the symptoms what must have happened. He alerted the authorities, and a post-mortem examination revealed the presence of a pint of greenish-blue liquid in his stomach. Mary was arrested and held in custody, and when put on trial at Exeter Assizes on 23 March 1819, she was convicted on a charge of murder. Several respected medical men had been called as witnesses to the fact that her husband had died in agony.

The verdict was a foregone conclusion. After the judge pronounced the death sentence, Mary shook her fist at her accusers, exclaiming defiantly that she would never forgive any of her persecutors: 'they have sworn false, and the devil will drag them into hell, and God will forgive me.' She was led away to the cells, muttering violently as she threw them all a last angry look.

At the same sessions, Smallacombe was convicted of passing a forged three-shilling piece at Mary Wood's St Thomas shop in Exeter on 25 February while attempting to buy some bread and cheese. On being searched, a forged shilling was found in his shoe, and a bottle of quicksilver in his pocket. He was given a sentence of one year, and was therefore in gaol at the time Mary Woodman went to the gallows. It was said that he had tried to get a witness to swear that Charles Woodman had purchased poison himself with the intention of committing suicide, but such was the reputation of both prisoners that nobody was prepared to perjure themselves by giving such evidence at the trial.

Also appearing before the courts at this session was Mary's 40-year-old brother, William. He was tried and charged with the 'indescribable offence' of bestiality but acquitted, although a fellow prisoner charged with the same thing, Joseph Atkins, was found guilty and hanged.

When she mounted the gallows with what appeared to be almost an act of defiance, Mary Woodman looked around her for a final view of Smallacombe, but to her dismay the authorities had taken steps to make sure that he was nowhere to be seen. Despite the entreaties of the prison chaplain, she refused to confess to her crime, but agreed to repeat the Lord's Prayer after him in an almost inaudible voice, before she was led to the noose. After her body had been left to hang, it was cut down and given to the surgeons for dissection.

8

'I LOVED HER TOO WELL TO MURDER HER!'

Torrington, 1822

In a small village like Torrington, news and gossip travelled fast, and little ever remained secret. During the autumn of 1821, it was widely known that 35-year-old Mary Stevens, spinster of the parish, was expecting the child of 19-year-old Philip Chappell. Both were employed by Mr Baget, a glover, Chappell in the manufacture of goods and Stevens as a servant. Neither of them were earning enough money to be able to support themselves and a new arrival, and they were not alone in wondering how they would solve the problem when the time came.

One day in November, Robert Vicary, a dyer, was chatting to Chappell and told him that 'it was a bad job that she was with child'. Chappell moodily agreed. When asked what he was going to do about it, he said he 'would not mind it if he was out of his time', in other words, if he was an adult.

'You have both good friends,' Vicary told him, 'and I dare say they would have no objection to maintain the child till you are out of your time, and you had better get married.'

Chappell retorted that he would 'be damned' if ever he married her, as what would he do with a wife when he was so young. Vicary said there was always a chance that the child she was carrying might be stillborn, and if so what would he give for such news? 'Five shillings,' was the terse answer.

As Mary became visibly larger, so their friends become increasingly concerned for them. On 6 December, Elizabeth Chambers saw Chappell on the other side of the street. She had assumed that he would be fulfilling his obligations, and was planning to marry Mary. When he waved to her in greeting, she stopped and called out to him, 'I suppose, Philip, you have made up the match?'

'I know nothing about it,' was his answer; 'come over, and I will tell you a bit about it.' Elizabeth said she was busy, and did not have the time to stop and talk. Another of her friends, Thomas Thorn, was with her, and Chappell crossed the street to join them.

'I suppose you intend to marry her,' Chambers continued, determined not to be fobbed off.

'I know nothing about marrying,' Chappell repeated.

Feeling that he had an obligation to face up to his responsibilities and make an honest woman of the future mother of his child, Elizabeth would not let the matter drop. She told him that she knew where he could go and buy things more cheaply, as they would need to set up home together. He received this unsolicited advice in sullen silence.

Next evening, a little after eight o'clock, Eliza Passmore of Castle Street was looking out of her window when she saw Mary Stevens on foot. Although it was dark at that time, there was a full moon, and there was no mistaking the heavily pregnant woman dressed in a grey cloak, white apron, black bonnet, and dark gown, walking towards the Castle Garden gate. It struck Eliza that Mary was looking unusually smart. A few minutes later Samuel Chambers saw Chappell in Castle Lane, and they exchanged a few friendly words before Chappell continued on his way down the lane to Castle Hill. Not long after that James Parminter was on the hill with his friend John Dingle, and as they passed the bowling green they noticed a man and a woman before them on Old Maid's Walk. They were probably the last people to see the couple together.

Early on the morning of 8 December, William Handford, a labourer, was walking past the mill leat at the bottom of the hill, and noticed a woman's body in the water, which was about eighteen inches deep. He called for assistance, and another man helped to haul her out, with the aid of a crook attached to her clothes. They noticed three wounds on the side of her head as they carried her to the side of a rock nearby.

They sent for a surgeon, and Thomas Vicary came to inspect the body. One of the dead woman's wounds, over the left eye, had been inflicted with considerable force, and cut deeply into the bone, while there was another incision about an inch and a half long by the right eye. He did not think either of these injuries could have caused death in themselves. Further examination revealed another small cut on her right hand. The body was removed to the town that afternoon for closer examination, Vicary examined the blows again, and said that they might have caused 'temporary stupefaction'. Once she had been thrown in the river she would have been unable to save herself, and drowned. Her body must have been lying there for several hours before it was discovered.

On 9 December, an inquest was held in the town before James Cutcliffe, the mayor and coroner. As if blindly resigned

Castle Hill, Torrington.

to his fate, Chappell had made no effort to flee from the village. He was arrested, charged with murder and sent to the county gaol at Exeter. Meanwhile, the same day, William Passmore, a local constable, searched the house of Chappell's parents, and found a pair of leather breeches in the bedroom, tied up in an apron. When he showed them to Chappell, the latter admitted they were his. He said he had got them dirty after digging for potatoes on a wet day, and he had washed them in the river.

When Chappell appeared at Exeter Assizes on 22 March, the courtroom was crowded. Chappell pleaded not guilty, but Mr Stevens, who outlined the case for the prosecution, had found several people to testify to their conversations with him in recent months and his refusal to marry the woman he was accused of having killed. Among them were Robert Vicary, Elizabeth Chambers and Eliza Passmore. Another employee of Mr Baget, Henry Lewis, recalled having seen Chappell on 7 December as he left their place of work at about eight o'clock, and returned on the following morning between ten and eleven o'clock. On coming in he sat down beside the stove and 'appeared in a very low way'. Though he did not say anything, within a few days Lewis realised the reason why.

When called to defend himself in front of the court, Chappell exclaimed loudly, 'My Lord, I am as innocent as anybody in the court; I loved her too well to murder her!' A few witnesses were called to give character references, and they all spoke of his 'general good conduct and gentle demeanour' up to the time of Mary Stevens' death.

It was not enough to save him. There could only be one possible outcome, and the jury did not take long to return a verdict of guilty. Throughout the trial Chappell had barely moved at all and listened to the proceedings impassively. As the judge passed sentence of death the prisoner broke down in tears, and as he was led away to the cells he walked with a trembling, unsteady step.

After a few hours of reflection, that evening he had a change of heart. He confessed to the minister that while taking that final walk with Mary, he was seized with desperation at the thought of their plight. Grabbing hold of a stick from the ground, he hit her several times on the head. He had never intended to kill her, and it had been done on impulse. Once he had attacked her, he realised that she must be dead, and threw her body into the water.

A large crowd gathered on the morning of 25 March at Exeter gaol to watch his execution. He was brought out of his cell shortly before midday, and, while the executioner was adjusting the rope and the prison chaplain was reading the prayers, he stared vacantly around him, paying little attention to either. After shaking hands with a couple of officials, he was duly 'launched into eternity'.

9

'PUT THEM OUT OF THE WAY AS SOON AS WE CAN'

Plymouth, 1830

John and Mary Fowell lived at William Street, Morice Town, Devonport. He was a sawyer in Devonport Dockyard, and they had two sons, William, aged 9, and John, aged 6.

They were well known in the area, and several neighbours suspected that Mary was not altogether 'in her right mind'. Their forebodings were soon to be sadly realised. On the evening of Friday, 29 October 1830, the boys' playmate, 10-year-old William Morrish, was at the house. Mary was sitting in a chair beside him, reading the Bible and talking to herself at intervals. The boys sat down with their cards, and a few minutes later Morrish's younger brother and two other boys from the same street came into the room. Although she had never previously shown any hostility to neighbours and their children coming into the house, something had evidently irritated Mary this time. She went to a cupboard, took out a hatchet, and threatened to 'chop them down' if they did not leave. William Morrish was allowed to stay, and after they had finished their game he went home. As he was leaving, Mary told her children to say goodnight to him. This was something she had never done before, and he felt it was rather odd.

The next morning he dropped in to ask what the time was, and to see the boys again. There was no sign of them. He noticed both beds, and above the larger there was a white sheet hanging down like a curtain, as if to conceal the bedding.

That same morning John Fowell was working as usual in the Dockyard. He generally started very early, and one of the boys would bring him his breakfast while he was there. This time his wife, who had not been seen in the yard for

Devonport, near the Dockyard gate.

several months, appeared with his food. They exchanged a few words, and she told him that their children were dead. What nonsense, her husband exclaimed. How could they be?

She then repeated the statement. If that was the case, he told her angrily, she must have killed them. She replied that a woman never killed children. He told her to go home at once, and he would follow her as soon as possible. As he went to change back into his everyday clothes, one of his colleagues, William Honeycomb, asked Mary gently whether either of the children had been ill. She told him that they had been unwell all night, and they both died early in the morning. As he knew, children 'often died suddenly'. She told her husband to stay where he was, because there was no point in him coming home. All he had to do was to tell her where Mr Garland the undertaker lived, so that she could go and arrange for him to provide the coffins. She asked Honeycombe if he would be kind enough to help and bury them the next day, for 'we want to put them out of the way as soon as we can'. As she was speaking, Honeycombe noticed that the colour of her lips changed from pale to 'besom' in colour, and she seemed strangely excited.

Later that morning, Mr and Mrs Fowell went into a shop run by Mary Willcocks, who lived in the same house as them. Mrs Willcocks had seen the children on Friday morning, and they had both been perfectly well at the time. John Fowell asked her whether she had seen the children that morning, and when she said she had not, he asked her if she would come back to the house and go upstairs with him. Mary accompanied them back to the house, but did not say anything until they had returned to the shop.

When Mr Fowell and Mrs Willcocks entered the house and pulled back the covers on the bed, they saw the children's bodies lying on their backs. Mrs Willcocks then asked Mrs Fowell why did she not come and call for help when she knew the children were so ill, but Mrs Fowell told her it would not have been of any use. On being asked again, she said that they had died at about four o'clock, adding that they had been groaning almost all night, and at four o'clock the Almighty 'had taken the breath out of them'. The room, she said, had been surrounded by angels all night.

A surgeon, Thomas Crossing, was called out, and when he examined the children, he concluded that they had died from suffocation. There were marks on the bodies, and when he asked Mary what had caused them, she said they were noisy and would not sleep, so she beat them with a cane. It was a good thing for poor people, she went on, when their children died. Her husband was most foolish to cry about it when he should have been glad, and if only he had allowed her more money, she would have found it easier to support them all.

An inquest was held at the Devonport workhouse on 1 November. Among the witnesses were William Honeycombe and Mary Willcocks, who said that when she was taken to see the children's bodies on Saturday morning she thought they had been dead for several hours. Though she did not immediately notice any signs of violence on their bodies, she saw what looked like the mark of a fingernail on John Fowell's neck, but was much too 'hurried' to say anything about it at the time. She referred to her fears that Mrs Fowell had not been in her right mind for some time, and that Mrs Fowell was sometimes kind, and sometimes without any apparent reason just the contrary. Thomas Crossing confirmed cause of death in both cases, saying that the two boys had died from suffocation by strangling. Ambrose Norsworthy and Richard Ellis, the two constables who had also been called to the house that morning, corroborated briefly what Mrs Fowell had said about their having died at four o'clock. The jury returned a verdict of wilful murder.

Mary Fowell went on trial at Exeter Assizes in March 1831, on a charge of wilfully murdering William Fowell by fixing her nails around his neck and strangling him. It was deemed easier by the court to proceed with one offence, rather than two, hence there was no mention in the charge of her killing her younger son John. The prisoner's appearance in the dock spoke for itself, with 'her wild, restless eyes, her haggard cheek and general demeanour' – the look of a woman who was not well and probably not accountable for her actions. When asked how she would plead, she answered, 'I am not guilty, I never touched him at any time.' The Clerk of Arraigns asked her if she objected to the jury as they stood up to be sworn, and she told him angrily that she would have no trial because she was not guilty.

During the court proceedings she continued to ramble at intervals, making inarticulate sounds. When cross-examined, she said rather incoherently that she had done it for the good of the children. The angels had told her three years ago to kill them, as they would be better off than they would be here on earth, although she did not wish them to go because she was a good deal happier with them than without them.

After the facts of the case had been outlined to the jury, Mary Willcocks was called as a witness. While she was giving her evidence, the prisoner interrupted her to say, 'I was led by the spirit; I was to do what was right and just, by myself.' When she was told to be quiet, she retorted, 'I must speak, there is no law in the kingdom to prevent my speaking.'

Everyone recognised she was mentally ill and had little if any responsibility for her actions. After the judge summed up briefly, the jury found her not guilty on the grounds of insanity. She was sentenced to be detained during His Majesty's pleasure.

10

'BETTER OR WORSE, I HAVE DONE IT ALL'

Plymouth, 1835

After Henry and Jane Honey married in June 1832, they lived with his parents and grandmother at King Street, Plymouth. Jane's mother was the landlady of the Rose and Crown public house in Old Town Street nearby. At the time of their wedding, he was only nineteen and his bride was three years younger. There had been some doubt on the part of his parents, if not her mother as well, as to their suitability for each other, and the ceremony took place without their knowledge. Once they were married, some thought they seemed contented enough with each other. Others who observed them more closely believed he was leading a dissolute life, carrying on with other women and drinking too much, and that their childless union was increasingly unhappy.

Old Town Street, Plymouth. (© Steve Johnson)

The Rose and Crown, Old Town Street, Plymouth. (© Steve Johnson)

King Street, Plymouth, c. 1955.

Matters soon went from bad to worse. Shortly after midnight on Sunday, 5 July 1835, Henry's mother and grandmother were awoken by loud shrieking. When they went to investigate, they found Jane lying on her back, covered in blood. Neighbours who had heard the noise entered the house to see if they could help, and moved her gently into an adjoining parlour. A physician and surgeon were summoned and arrived within a few minutes. Jane's throat was bleeding profusely, and they pressed it together to try and staunch the flow of blood. She rallied slightly, uttered a few barely coherent words, and lapsed into unconsciousness.

Meanwhile, her husband was lying in another room in the house, his hands and shirtsleeves stained with blood. It was evident that he had attacked Jane and run through the passage to the adjoining house for assistance, but the neighbours led him back. A trail of blood along the passage and outside the front door told its own story. He subsequently dosed himself with laudanum in an attempt to take his own life, but it merely made him drowsy. The police were called and Constable Nathaniel Millett took Henry to the Guildhall. As he was led away, he asked whether there was any hope for his wife's life. 'No, it is no use to flatter you,' said Millett, 'the case is fatal.' 'Better or worse, I have done it all,' he admitted. As people stood around watching, he said, 'You may look at me; I have been a fool to myself, she have [sic] driven me to do what I have done.' Once in custody, he was locked up with two officers, who kept watch to prevent any further suicide attempts.

When the surgeon Charles Hingston arrived, he was shown into the back parlour, and found Jane lying on her back. He applied his hand gently to her throat, and she revived a little, asking feebly for her mother-in-law, who came and kissed her forehead. About five minutes later she breathed her last, just as her husband came in and admitted responsibility. Hingston conducted the post-mortem examination, at which he confirmed that she had died from haemorrhage and suffocation.

An inquest was opened at 6 o'clock that evening, at the Coach and Horses Inn, a few doors down from the Honeys' home, and continued over the next two days. At his own request, Honey was brought from the prison into the inquest room, as a vast crowd of curious onlookers, ever eager for any kind of show, had come to catch a sight of this apparent monster in human form. Several 'medical gentlemen' provided evidence that the victim had died after her husband had deliberately cut her throat with a razor. It was also stated that Henry had not only taken laudanum, but had been 'for some time in a state of extraordinary excitement in consequence of excessive drinking and irritation at being accused of keeping company with the wife of another man'. His own mother and other witnesses, possibly keen to try and spare him from the gallows, were ready to cast doubts on his sanity.

When the witnesses' evidence was concluded on 7 July, the coroner reminded the jury that the habitual drunkenness of an individual in such a case was no extenuation, but merely heightened the offence. If they believed the prisoner to be 'a lunatic and distracted', it was their duty to say so. He hoped they would merely consider the evidence which had been given on oath, and not be influenced by anything they may have heard out of court. The jury retired for just over an hour, before returning a verdict of wilful murder.

While in custody at Plymouth, Honey was 'in a very desponding state'. At first he spoke little and ate nothing, and a round-the-clock guard to prevent him from taking his own life was maintained. Later that week, after receiving visits at his own request from a local curate, a Unitarian minister, and the vicar, he was taken to Exeter gaol to await trial later in the month.

Jane Honey's funeral took place at the Ebenezer Wesleyan Chapel in Plymouth on 11 July. Among those attending were Henry's parents, sisters and brothers, as well as Jane's two sisters and two brothers. As the coffin was lowered into the ground after the service, Mr and Mrs Honey and one of Jane's sister, fainted and all three had to be helped into a nearby house to recover. The newspapers which reported the event also noted in a separate paragraph that the murderer in his cell at Exeter had asked the officer watching him to bring him some milk and water. After drinking it, he sighed, 'Oh, that I had drank nothing stronger than this.'

The case came to trial on 31 July under Mr Justice Coleridge, with Mr Rowe appearing for the prosecution and Mr Praed for the defence. Honey pleaded not guilty, and was offered a chair to sit on while in the dock. At first he declined, but as the proceedings lengthened, he sat down.

The first witness for the prosecution was Elizabeth Daniel, who lived in Cambridge Street. She said that Henry Honey had been to her house on the Saturday afternoon, the day before the murder, in a furious temper, saying she had called on his wife and told her that he had been caught *in flagrante delicto* with Mrs Smith, who lived in Mrs Daniel's house. When she firmly denied it, he said he would return home and ask Jane who had been spreading the story around; if she would not tell him, 'he would be the death of her'. He was so angry that she suspected he might have been drinking, particularly as he 'flung his hands about' when he spoke, but his speech was perfectly coherent.

Mary Warner, a former servant of the prisoner's father, said she had often seen husband and wife together and occasionally saw him 'in liquor', but as a rule they seemed quite happy together. She recalled the events of Saturday afternoon. Jane Honey was in the wash-house when her husband came home drunk. A furious Jane told him he had just been in Cambridge Street, presumably with another woman. When he explained that he had

John Taylor Coleridge, Mr Justice Coleridge.

only been to tell Mrs Smith that she had to go and get her husband's tea, she told him angrily he was a 'good for nothing blackguard' who had 'been with the damned whores again'. He denied it, and invited her to go to Cambridge Street with him so he could prove her wrong.

'I'm damned if I do go,' she retorted. He then asked Mrs Warner to go with him, and she agreed. When they arrived there Mrs Daniel, Mrs Smith and several other neighbours were on the stairs. Looking at Mrs Daniel, Mr Honey asked Mrs Warner, 'Is that the woman?' Mrs Warner said she did not think so, as she thought she was differently dressed. Then Mrs Daniel, looking at Mr Honey, said firmly, 'I hope you are perfectly satisfied it was not me who told your wife.'

'I'll go home and find out the author before I go to bed,' Henry said threateningly. Turning to Mrs Warner, he said that if she did not tell him who had been telling such falsehoods about him to his wife, 'you shall never put foot inside our door again.'

Mrs Warner and Henry then left the house for a few minutes while Jane Honey, her mother-in-law and mother Mrs King stayed behind. Then Mrs King told her daughter that she had received an anonymous letter about Henry. He asked her to hand him the note but she refused, saying she would give it to her daughter instead. Jane took it, and she and her mother went into the kitchen. When Mrs Warner returned about five minutes later, she found an angry Mrs King saying that she was damned if her daughter was going to have to put up with this any longer, and threatening to take her away on the Monday morning. Jane taxed her husband for his misbehaviour but he denied everything, saying it was 'all lies', and he had never even spoken to another girl since he had been married.

'I won't stand it any longer,' he said to his mother-in-law, adding that she was welcome to take her daughter away with her. Jane muttered something angrily, which Mrs Warner did not hear, and Mr Honey left the house, saying he would go and fetch Mr and Mrs Smith. When he returned, Mr Smith was with him, saying he had come down to 'clear' Mr Honey. The latter said he was perfectly satisfied, and thanked Mr Smith for coming. They all sat down amicably to supper together, and when Mr Honey said he would see Mr Smith to the door, Jane told him that she intended to go out as well. To this Henry raised no objection.

Mr Honey and Mr Smith left the house together, but Mrs Warner stayed at home. Henry returned at about ten o'clock that evening, somewhat the worse for drink, and fell down in the passage. Picking himself up, he went upstairs, and asked 'Jenny' to bring him a light from the kitchen. Later that evening he was downstairs again and Mrs King returned briefly, then she left the house with Mrs Warner at about eleven o'clock, as Jane was going upstairs to bed.

On Sunday morning Mrs Warner returned to the house shortly before midday, as Mary Honey was standing at the front door. As she was entering, Mrs Warner clearly heard Jane calling out angrily from the bedroom, 'I shan't – I won't – I'm damned if I don't.' Next Mary Honey ran up the stairs to ask about some dirty clothes that the servant needed to wash. After that Mrs Warner crossed the street to return home, but had only taken a few steps before she heard Mary Honey screaming. She turned round to see Jane staggering out of Mrs Oliver's door, next to the Honeys' house. She heard a violent knocking on the door, which remained firmly shut, and saw young William Oliver looking out of the window. Next she saw Mary Honey running to her daughter, who collapsed into her arms.

Henry Honey then ran out of the house in his shirtsleeves, took hold of his wife from his shocked mother-in-law, and helped her into the passage with the aid of his own mother. They put her on the stairs while they opened the back parlour door. She saw soap lather on Henry Honey's face but did not notice anything on his shirtsleeves until he took hold of his wife, at which point she saw blood halfway up his sleeves. He then ran up the stairs saying, 'Stop – stop, I'll soon do it,' went to his bedroom and she heard the door being shut. Immediately afterwards he came down again, saying he had taken laudanum and was about to die. Mrs Warner followed him as he went into the kitchen and asked her for a drink of cold water, which she gave him. He then fell to his knees, saying that 'she can't be saved.' Mrs Warner told him that there was hope, and his wife could be saved. He then struck his breast like a madman, went into the back parlour where Jane's body had been laid, and then went upstairs.

The next witness was William Sergeant, of the North Country Pink, a public house on the Barbican. He remembered being in the tap room at about 6 o'clock on the morning of Sunday 5 July, when the prisoner came in and asked for a glass of port. He took him one and he drank it, then asked for directions to a barber's shop. Sergeant told him where to find one just up the street. A few minutes later he returned and asked for a noggin of brandy. Honey then told him it was about half past midnight when he got back home on Saturday night. He said he had knocked down his wife, after being told about an anonymous letter that had been sent to Mrs King, accusing him of having an affair with another married woman, when at the time he was drinking with the woman's husband, after returning from the house of Mr Windeatt, where he had been repairing a piano. He told Sergeant that before this letter arrived, he and his wife had 'lived very comfortably' together. He said also that she had behaved very kindly to him since the quarrel, when she found that instead of being with the wife, he was drinking with the husband. He also told him that he had been to a shop and purchased a new bonnet to be trimmed and sent home to his wife, and that he had seen it at home when he left the house that morning. He asked Mr Sargent for a boat, and was told he would find plenty outside. Henry went out and came in again with a waterman, and asked for a glass of the best brandy, while the waterman had a pint of beer. He then left the pub and returned ten minutes later with two watermen, for whom he ordered a glass of rum each, and he had some more brandy in a tumbler, to which he added water. When he left, Sargent said, he seemed sober.

Elizabeth Coates, who hed been a lodger at Mr Honey's father's house, said Henry and Jane had always seemed 'very comfortable together', as long as he was sober. She was aware of occasional small differences between them, but no major quarrels, though when he was drunk he could never bear to be contradicted, and during the few days before Jane's death, he had been drinking to excess. She heard him go out of the house on Sunday morning while Jane and her mother-in-law were having breakfast together, and Jane appeared perfectly composed as both women, plus Mrs Coates, left the house about eleven o'clock that morning, Jane in her Sunday best. As they walked up King Street towards Jane's mother's house, she pointed out her husband coming down the street towards them, dirty, dishevelled, and apparently drunk. Jane's manner was rather distant, and as he passed them, she refrained from speaking to him at first. When he asked her where she was going, Mrs Coates answered on her behalf, telling him coldly that his wife was going to see her mother. He ordered Jane to turn back, and took her by the arm. She glared at him, told him how dirty he was, and asked where he had been. He told her he had been to Bovisand by the Breakwater, and when she said she did not believe him, he showed her his hands, which were red and heated as if he had just been rowing. All four walked on without any further conversation until they came to the next public house where he left them, and went in.

Later Mrs Coates and Jane went back to the Honey's house. Jane went upstairs and brought her husband's clothes into the kitchen. Shortly afterwards he returned, and Jane called to him from the kitchen, telling him he did not need to go upstairs as she had just brought his clothes down for him. He said he wanted to go up anyway, and about five minutes later Mrs Coates heard him call out for Jane. He told her he wanted her, but she snapped back that she would not come. A couple of minutes later she changed her mind and went upstairs, and Mrs Coates heard conversation in raised voices. Mary Honey said she would go upstairs and see what they wanted. Some discussion then ensued about laundry and various family matters, after which Mary came downstairs, and everything was quiet for another five minutes or so – until Mrs Coates heard a loud scream, which she recognised as Jane's voice. She then heard Jane running downstairs with her husband in pursuit, his heavy boots making a considerable noise. She ran from the kitchen into the nearby wash-house and shut the door.

Henry Honey then ran into the passage, shouting that his wife had cut her throat. Mrs Coates went into the passage and saw Mrs Honey carrying her daughter, bleeding profusely with her hand against her neck.

William Oliver, the Honeys' neighbour in King Street, then took the stand to say that at around half twelve on 5 July, he heard a violent knocking at his front door, followed by a shriek. He looked out of the window to see Jane Honey trying to get to the doorstep, with her mother-in-law running after her and asking what she had done. Jane then fell into her mother-in-law's arms, as her husband came and took hold of her, and only then did the wound in her throat become clearly visible. As Oliver went next door to see if he could help, Honey carried his wife into the kitchen, his mother followed them and ordered him to get a doctor. Jane's body lay in the back parlour, while her husband sat in a chair, saying, 'I've done it, and it cannot be undone.' Several times he asked, 'is that my dear Jane; is that my dear wife?' As he did so, said Oliver, he 'appeared in a great agony of mind, throwing his hands about in a distracted state, and rubbing them across his breast.'

The final witness for the prosecution was Henry's mother, Mary. She recalled her son and daughter-in-law returning home shortly before midday on Sunday 5 July, but beyond remembering that Jane had told her husband to hurry up and put on his shirt, as he was 'as maz'd as a sheep,' she said nothing of consequence, let alone anything about hearing screams or seeing any violence taking place.

After this the judge invited the prisoner to retire while the court briefly adjourned. When they reassembled, Honey said that he did not have sufficient strength to address the jury, and instead he had written down a statement that he wanted to be read aloud. In it he confessed to the killing, 'but denied everything like premeditation or malice, attributing it to forgetfulness at the moment, and accident'. He said that while he was shaving, there was an argument between himself and his wife about her plans to visit her mother without waiting for him to get dressed so he could accompany her. He asked her to wait, but she slipped behind him towards the door. Trying to stop her, and forgetting that he had a razor in his hand, he stretched out his arm, which encircled her neck. She shrieked as she struggled to get away from him. He threw the razor away, and pursued her downstairs. While admitting that he had said the words attributed to him by the witnesses, he denied the construction which had been put upon them.

At 2.10 p.m. the judge began his address to the jury, recommending that according to what they had heard, they might return a charge of manslaughter, a verdict they only needed to consider for a couple of minutes. Turning to Henry Honey, he said he hoped that 'you really feel all that bitterness of remorse which must spring up in the minds of all but the most unfeeling and hardened, at the thought that must ever be present with you of the heinous crime you have committed.' He had been guilty 'of a crime of a very deep dye, yet the law spares your life.' His sentence would be 'to be removed from your native land for ever' – transportation for life.

11

'THAT WILL STOP THE OLD WOMAN FROM HALLOOING'

Tedburn St Mary, 1847

In her younger days Grace Holman had been a servant at Great Fulford, a magnificent mansion near Dunsford. She had been married twice, first to a Mr Hetherton, by whom she had one son, a builder who was living in London. During her second marriage to Mr Holman, a local farmer, she had a son and two daughters (one deceased four years earlier), both of whom also married local farmers. Long since retired, 80 years old and increasingly frail, yet still fiercely independent, Grace lived on her own at Taphouse, Tedburn St Mary. Her home was one of two semi-detached cottages, the other being occupied by William Collins and his wife. They had become friends as well as good neighbours, and in view of her advancing years they were very conscientious about keeping an eye on her and ensuring she had all she needed.

At about six o'clock on the evening of Saturday, 2 December 1847, William Orchard, a thatcher who lived nearby, and another old friend of Grace's for many years, came to the cottage and had tea with her. He was the last person to see her alive.

Next door, after a long and busy day, William Collins went to bed at about eight o'clock that evening. At around midnight he was awoken briefly by a sound, as if someone was moving the latch of his front door, but he thought it must be just a stray animal pressing up against it. As he heard nothing more, he went back to sleep. On Sunday morning he was up soon after seven o'clock, a little later than his wife, also Grace. When he came downstairs, she told him that somebody had done something to the door and she was unable to get outside. He was about to investigate when she looked out of the window, and saw a girl in the opposite field pulling turnips. They recognised her as Elizabeth Hall, and called her to come and see whether she could open the door from outside. Elizabeth found that a rope had been tied to the guard of the latch of the door with a gimlet, which she removed and handed to them.

Tedburn St Mary. (© Derek Harper)

At about eight o'clock, Nathaniel Beer was coming down from Taphouse towards Westwater when he saw William. The latter told him what had happened, and that somebody must have tried to break in. The previous evening, only a mile or two away, another farmhouse had been entered by several men who looted the cupboards and left with a large haul of goods. Both men decided to go and check on Mrs Holman to make sure she was all right. They noticed that a pane of glass had been taken from the casement of the spare room. When they knocked on the front door but received no answer, they checked the outside catch and found it was unlocked.

It was gradually dawning on them that whoever had broken into Mrs Holman's house had tried to prevent anybody from raising the alarm by fastening a gimlet pierced through the doorpost and door of the adjacent cottage and running a cord or small rope through the guard of the latch. This would have been enough to prevent anybody wishing to leave. The thieves then tried to reach the window of Mrs Holman's bedroom, by climbing along a plum tree growing against the wall of the house. They reached the window, but could not enter as the casement was so small, and oak bars blocked their way. From the garden immediately in front of the cottage, they had taken a fir pole which had been used as a prop for an apple tree. The upper part of which had been sawn off, as if to form a resting place for the foot, and placed it against the house underneath the spare bedroom window. This was enough to enable one person to get in, go downstairs to the kitchen, and let the other in through the front door, which was evidently what had happened.

When they went upstairs to the bedroom the first thing Collins and Beer saw were boxes and drawers scattered and opened on the floor, then they looked at the bed, on top of which a box and chair had been thrown. To their horror, they realised that Mrs Holman must be underneath. Mr Beer removed the items, gently turned the bedclothes down, and discovered her lying on her left side with her hand against her head. Though the body was not yet cold, he could feel no pulse and she was obviously dead.

Investigations shortly afterwards suggested that the house had been burgled after Grace was killed. A set of at least twelve silver teaspoons engraved with the initials GW and two pairs of silver sugar tongs – one plain, one twisted – some money and a shawl were all taken. Footmarks indicated that one of the men wore shoes or boots nailed with small hobs, the other a narrow and probably new pair.

Collins and Beer then went to report her death to Baldwin Fulford, a magistrate who lived nearby. Fulford had known the deceased very well, as she had been a servant in his father's family for many years. His brother, a retired army captain, joined him as they went to her house to view her body and the footmarks left by the intruders as described by Beer. Fulford took charge of her papers, made examinations of witnesses who were around, and circulated information to police in neighbouring communities so that anybody behaving suspiciously could be apprehended.

An inquest was opened later in the day at the Red Lion Inn, Taphouse. Fulford was in charge of the proceedings. The main witnesses called were William Collins, Nathaniel Beer, and William Orchard, who testified to having had tea with her late the previous afternoon, and to her having locked her front door after he left. Another of Grace Holman's friends of long standing, Jane Langdon, spoke of having visited Grace's house every week as a child, and regularly helping her with small jobs.

Herman Holman (no relation to Mrs Holman), a surgeon at Crediton, who had attended her regularly for the last ten years, confirmed she had been very frail. When he conducted the post-mortem examination he found the face very much distorted, swollen and discoloured. There was an indented mark across the neck, which made him think she had been subjected to some heavy weight. Death had been caused by a pressure preventing the passage of air through the windpipe, probably caused by strangulation or suffocation. She had suffered from respiratory problems for some time, and any slight pressure on her chest would have been sufficient to kill her.

Although the area was sparsely populated, all the local police forces cast a net from which it would be increasingly hard for the guilty party to escape. A few days later, three suspicious individuals were arrested, taken into custody and examined at an enquiry held over three days (17-19 January 1849) at a private examination at Exeter Castle before the magistrates. The men were James Landick, James Mills (also known as Summers) and Henry Woods (also known as 'Cockney Harry'). Landick and Mills were both travelling cutlers, who also made a little money by more dubious means. The latter, who came from Tavistock, was the son of the sexton, a well respected man of the area, but his son had fallen into bad company. Henry Woods initially gave the impression of being half-witted. However, it soon became apparent that an idiot's exterior masked a shrewd brain, more than capable of playing the idiot when it suited his purposes. Unlike the others, he came from a good family, had been well educated, and formerly worked in an attorney's office with a view to following a legal career. He was a cunning idler who found that living on the wrong side of the law could prove more lucrative if he was prepared to take up 'a vagabond wandering mode of life', and was careful enough to stay one step ahead of the dubious company with whom he became involved.

The party had met at Moretonhampstead, where they hatched the scheme to break into Mrs Holman's cottage and rob her. At about nine o'clock on the evening of 2 December they left the town, reaching the cottage about two and a half hours later. Landick entered the house through the bedroom window and let the others into the house. Once they had secured the door of the Collins' cottage, rendering disturbance less likely – at least until they had had time to make their getaway – they blacked their faces at the foot of the stairs and went to Mrs Holman's bedroom. When she showed signs of stirring, Mills pulled the bedclothes over her head, and kept her in that position, sitting on the bed beside her so she could not move.

Meanwhile, Landick was breaking open every locked drawer and box in the house he could find, and being frustrated in not finding the large haul of cash expected, he went to Grace's bedside and demanded to know where she kept it. She said she had none, but he retorted that she must have a good deal. He continued searching, and in the window he found a purse containing a sovereign, four halfcrowns, and five shillings. In another drawer which he had broken open, he found some silver spoons and a crooked sixpence. He took the spoons, then went downstairs and in a basin in a cupboard found yet more spoons, then returned to the bedroom and asked her again where she was keeping her money. She insisted desperately that everything she had was in her purse. Mills moved off the bed, and Landrick seized a box of clothes, which he threw over her.

'Don't, for God's sake, you will kill her!' Woods cried out.

'That will stop the old woman from hallooing,' Landick said callously.

They stayed in the house for almost three hours, searching in vain for any more valuables, then washed their faces and returned to Moretonhampstead. As they went, Landick gave Woods 12s as his share of the spoils. Later, on a patch of land outside the village, Landick wrapped the spoons in a piece of paper and buried them.

Woods, who now turned Queen's Evidence against his accomplices, was taken to the spot a few days later. Careful examination revealed an area where the ground had recently been disturbed, and it was dug over, but nothing was found. When Woods was questioned further on the subject, he replied, 'Dog rob dog,' suggesting that any booty had been concealed but his accomplices must have secretly removed it. In a scene of recrimination which afterwards ensued, the other two prisoners charged Woods with being a 'pretty informer', who himself 'was the person who pushed the handkerchief into the old woman's mouth, and but for that she would not have died.' Landick and Mills were then committed for trial at the next Exeter Assizes.

Landick had evidently dug up the spoons and brought them into Moretonhampstead. He gave them to Joseph Mills, who went to Bodmin with two accomplices, William Cann of Crediton, and Mary Ann Emery, and offered the spoons for sale. The person to whom they were offered informed the police, and they were taken into custody at Bodmin Gaol. When the full story emerged, Mills, Cann and Emery were taken to Exeter Gaol. Emery, aged only 20 but in poor health, was in no state to survive her ordeal. She died on 30 January.

Landick and Mills were brought to trial on 23 March at Exeter, before the Hon. Justice Williams, with Mr Greenwood and Mr Bevan as counsel for the prosecution, Robert Collier and John Karslake acting for the defence. The spoons were identified as Mrs Holman's property. After Mr Greenwood had stated the facts of the case without needing to call on any witnesses, Collier addressed the jury, contending that Woods's evidence had failed to incriminate Mills. He suggested that it was beyond doubt Woods had been party to the murder of a defenceless elderly woman, and in informing on the others had merely taken the rope from around his own neck in order to twist it around theirs. Moreover, the evidence against Landick and Mills was based on the word of someone unreliable. It would be impossible to satisfy the jury that they could believe one word that he had said, and as the case for the prosecution wholly rested on his evidence; both prisoners were therefore entitled to an acquittal.

After Mr Justice Williams had summed up, the jury acquitted Mills, but found Landick guilty, with a strong recommendation to mercy. When they were asked on what grounds, they said that they did not believe that he had planned to murder his victim. Nevertheless Mr Justice Williams passed sentence of death. In a later age, the defence counsel might have been able to argue more successfully that there was no evidence of premeditation, but Grace Holman had been treated quite brutally in the course of a burglary during which at least one of the offenders had shown neither mercy nor scruple towards her.

In the meantime, it had come to light that Landick had a long record of misdemeanours to his name. He had been imprisoned on several previous occasions for burglary, and in June 1848 a married couple living in a cottage in Ilsington had been robbed. Two other men, John Steer and William Pengelly, had been arrested and tried in connection with the case but acquitted as there was some doubt as to their identity. Now, under sentence of death and having nothing to lose, Landick confessed that he and a gypsy whom he had engaged as his accomplice were the guilty party all along.

He was executed by William Calcraft on 9 April.

12

'I BE LIKE ONE TIPSY'

Buckland Brewer, 1850

When Grace Parsons' husband left her and their daughter Maria, they found themselves without any means of support in their house at Bideford, and had no option but to enter the local union workhouse. Conditions in such institutions were almost without exception very harsh, in order that the able-bodied poor should not be too dependent on them. Those unfortunate enough to be sent there were usually treated little better than prisoners, often feeling that they were being punished for the crime of poverty. The able-bodied were made to work at such menial tasks as stonebreaking and crushing bones, as well as the routine tasks of cleaning and keeping the place tidy. Pauper children, as they were known, could be sent away or apprenticed without the permission or even knowledge of their parents. For some of them, this was to be welcomed as a means of escape.

In rural areas such as north Devon, from time to time farmers and their wives would visit the workhouse, and the more healthy children there would be recommended to them if thought suitable to go into service. When Robert and Sarah Bird needed an extra servant to help them on their farm at Buckland Brewer, it was the obvious place to look. Sarah went to the workhouse on 29 September 1849 and her choice fell on Maria, then aged about 14. Taking new clothes supplied by the union, Maria welcomed being able to leave. Sarah Bird had seemed kindly enough, and even if she anticipated a life of drudgery ahead of her, she hoped that her employers would be kindly people who would look after her well in return for working hard and doing all that was expected of her. During the rest of her short life, she was to be cruelly disappointed.

It was heartrending for Grace Parsons to say goodbye to her daughter, but she put on a brave face and looked forward to hearing about Maria's progress at the farm. The authorities at the workhouse were also obliged to keep a similar interest and ensure that she was in good hands, although some were more diligent in this aspect than others. Nevertheless, it appears that Thomas Surman at the Bideford Union was one of the more conscientious masters. About a month later Mrs Bird visited him, and told him the girl was making good progress. When she met Mrs Parsons in November, she said the same thing.

By the New Year, it was a very different situation. On 4 January 1850, Mrs Bird came to the union, said that Miss Parsons was dead, and asked if she could have a coffin for her. Mr Surman told Mrs Parsons, who was naturally horrified and thoroughly shaken by the news. She asked if she could go to the Birds' house next day to see her child for the last time. When she arrived, she saw the body laid out on a bed, partly covered with a sheet. As it was turned over, extensive injuries were clearly visible. From hip to ankle there were stripes, indicating severe punishment.

At an inquest, evidence was given that Maria had been brutally beaten by Mr and Mrs Bird, and the jury returned a verdict of wilful murder against them both. They appeared at Exeter Assizes before Mr Justice Talfourd on 22 March, with Mr Rowe and Mr Marshall acting as counsel for the prosecution, and Mr Slade and Mr Cox for the defence.

The first witness, Grace Parsons, told the court that on 4 January she had gone to visit Mrs Bird, who told her that her daughter had 'very dirty habits'. When she went upstairs she found her daughter's body in Mr Bird's bed, with a handkerchief tied round her arm. She asked what had been going on, and Mrs Bird said she had taken to lying down in her clothes. When she remarked to Mr Bird what a terrible state her child was in, with a black eye and marks on her face, he did not reply.

Mrs Bird asked her whether there would be a jury (an inquest) on the child, and Mrs Parsons said that was unlikely. Mr Bird told her that he had found the child dead on the morning of 29 December. Mrs Bird said that on the night before, when she was upstairs, Maria called out for water, and came down to the kitchen to fetch some. She had fallen down twice, and after the second time she said, 'I do not know what is the matter with me, I be like one tipsy, but I am not, am I?' She was told to go back upstairs. When Mr and Mrs Bird went up later, Maria called out. Mrs Bird lifted her out of bed, and as she did so, Maria's arm broke. When she asked Maria how she was, she said she was very sleepy, and when all was quiet she thought she would be able to sleep for a while. Mrs Bird went back downstairs but went back up later to check on the child. The latter complained that she was very cold, so Mrs Bird brought a bowl of hot water up with which to wash and warm her.

Later still, she told Mr Bird to go and check on Maria, as she seemed so quiet. He went to see her and said that she looked 'very smiling', but completely still. Mrs Bird went back to see for herself, and spoke to an elderly man who was sleeping in the same room as the child. He said he thought she was dead, as he had spoken to her several times and she had not answered. Mrs Bird then gave Grace a glass of wine.

On Saturday 6 January, Mrs Parsons returned, finding Mr Turner, the surgeon, upstairs. Grace was called up to identify her daughter's body, and was then told to leave the room. Mrs Bird persistently asked her not to have a jury on the child, and if she did not, Mrs Bird would be her friend as long as she lived. Grace rightly said that she 'could not give it up at all'; meaning that she could not give any such commitment to what was in effect perverting the course of justice. As she sat by the fire, Mrs Bird fell upon her knees, begging her 'dear Grace' for forgiveness, imploring her, 'Think on me and my poor dear children.' When Grace remained obdurate, Mr Bird joined in the argument on his wife's behalf; 'What's the use of having a jury on the child now! Look at the expense of it.' Grace Parsons assured them that they should 'never mind that', as the expense would not fall on either of them. Now aware that she and her husband would be unable to escape the legal processes as a result of the child having died while in their care, Mrs Bird admitted brokenly that she had been at fault by flogging the child.

Under cross-examination, Grace said that her child had been in service before. She was in the union, and Mrs Bird told her on the Friday she was welcome to bring anybody she knew to see the child. She admitted she was at fault for not having sent for a doctor, 'but they were their own doctor, and never had one for themselves'.

The next witness was Elizabeth Pedlar, who had known Maria Parsons, testified to the child having been in the best of health when she left the union, with no marks on her body, and that she was 'very clean in her habits, and was well conducted'.

Mary Branch, the wife of a Bideford blacksmith, went on 5 January to lay out the body of the child. When she undressed the body, she saw cuts from the ankle to the middle of the thigh, all covered in blood, a violent blow on the back of the hip, and further bruising above the waist. Going downstairs, she confronted Mrs Bird in the kitchen, asking her, 'How came you to serve the child so?' Panic-stricken, the latter led her up to her bedroom, and told her she would be a friend to her as long as she lived, if she would promise her that the mother of the child would say nothing about it.

'Why had you not sent for the doctor?' Mrs Branch asked. Mrs Bird shook her head helplessly as she admitted she was at fault for not having done so. 'I think you were,' said Mrs Branch.

'Will you do what I am going to ask you?' Mrs Bird pleaded. 'I will be a friend to you as long as I live, for one word of yours will go a great way.'

'Well, Mrs Bird, I cannot,' was Mrs Branch's answer, 'for I have seven children of my own, and my conscience will not let me.'

After that they went downstairs. Mrs Bird said Maria had called downstairs to her little boy for something to drink. Mrs Bird said, 'Come down yourself; do you want a servant to attend you?' The child came downstairs, slipped and fell. Mrs Bird took her by the arm, but she said she could get up herself, and appeared as if drunk. When cross-examined, she said to Mrs Bird that there was the mark of a blow on the head, and she said, 'That must have been a tumble.'

Mr Surman from the union said that when he asked Mrs Bird about a month after Maria had left the union how the girl was behaving, Mrs Bird told him that she was one of the best children she had ever had in the house. On a subsequent occasion she spoke in equally glowing terms of the child. However, when he saw Mrs Bird on Christmas Eve, she told him that the girl had taken to stealing and telling lies. He asked her if she had properly corrected her, and said that if he had been in her place he would not keep her in the house another night, but send her back. Mr Bird came to him on the morning of 4 January, and told him that she was dead. 'Dead – when did she die?' he asked. He said that at about two o'clock that morning he attended to her and she looked as if she was asleep, but three hours later he went to her room and found her dead.

William Johns, who lived about a mile from the Birds, was working on the farm on 5 November, and heard Mrs Bird scolding the girl. He caught mention of the words 'pig's mash', followed by blows, and the sound of the girl crying. When Maria came out she was carrying swine feed in her hand, and there was blood on her face. She spoke to him and showed him her arm, which had marks on it that looked as if they had been made by a stick, as well as a mark across her neck. As far as he knew, there was nobody else in the house apart from Mrs Bird. Another farm labourer, Richard Hopper, saw Maria around mid-December, and again on Boxing Day in the swill house, and thought she looked very unwell. On the second occasion he noticed her bleeding from a cut at the back of her head. When he saw Mrs Bird come out of the house where the girl was, and she told the girl to go in, he noticed bruises on the girl's arm and shoulders. On previous occasions he had seen both Mr and Mrs Bird beat her with a stick across her shoulders, reducing her to tears. He had seen thongs in the house tied on to a stick, which were now in the possession of the constable.

When cross-examined, he said he had seen Mr Bird strike Maria because she had not lit the fire. A pair of thongs were produced in court, and Hopper confirmed that they were the same ones he had seen in the house. Other witnesses corroborated this evidence.

Charles Colville Turner, a surgeon at Bideford, said that on Friday 4 January, Bird asked him to go and see a girl he had at his house. When Turner asked what the matter was with her, Bird said she was dead. The surgeon said it was a waste of his time coming immediately and deferred his visit until the next day, when he saw the child's body, and had it stripped. There were several wounds on the legs and thighs, apparently inflicted by some rough or irregular weapon, possibly even a brick, as well as bruises on the chest and collarbone, and discoloration of the face, plus wounds and abscesses on the arms and fingers. The skin over the bowels was discoloured, and the bruises on the arms looked about a fortnight old. There were two abscesses on the left arm, the nails on some of the fingers on the left hand appeared to have been gone for some time, the bone of the middle finger was protruding, and on the right arm above the elbow was another recently burst abscess. When the body was turned over, on the right hip was a large mark the size of the palm of the hand. On the posterior part of the hips were several wounds, which had been inflicted some time previously and were covered with plaster, with some bruising on the shoulder. The outer layer of the skin of the back was separated from the inner, the result of the blood having poured out between the two layers of skin after death. He thought she must have been dead for several days, and the cold weather would have prevented or delayed any decomposition.

Turner then made a post-mortem examination. There was a good deal of blood on the head, and discoloration of the skin from the forehead down the cheek. On removing the scalp he found another bruise on the back part of the head, and on removing the skull he fund the membrane of the brain congested, but the skull was perfectly sound. He examined the chest, the contents of which were healthy, apart from a slight adhesion of the right lung to the side. The stomach was empty, and the different organs were healthy. Death had been caused by external injuries to the head, but he could not say exactly how the blows had been inflicted. The child must have been in a gravely weakened condition, and her nervous system would have been affected accordingly. The nails might have been lost through frostbite, while a fall might have produced the mark on the hip, as a congestion of the brain coming on from natural causes would make a person giddy, and thus likely to fall. At this point the judge said he considered the internal appearances were the result of external injury.

The final witness for the prosecution, John Bird, an Exeter surgeon, said that a fall against a fender would have produced a wound on the head. The bruise on the hip might have been caused by a kick from a cow.

Addressing the court on behalf of Mr and Mrs Bird, Mr Slade asked the jury not to jump to the conclusion that the prisoners were guilty merely because of the evidence of medical testimony. Any blows on the child, he contended, were of so trifling in nature that no possible injury could have resulted from them, and the prisoners had been justified in administering them. As proof of their kindness to her, he said that the girl was clearly suffering from some disease, and they had attended to her with every care possible during the night. She had fallen down in the kitchen, and her head had probably hit the fender, thus hastening incipient congestion of the brain. Under these circumstances he believed the prisoners were entitled to an acquittal.

Mr Justice Talfourd then asked Mr Rowe what he wanted to tell the jury as to the cause of death. Medical testimony indicated that death was caused by a blow on the head, and not the injuries on the rest of the body. What evidence was there that either of the prisoners had inflicted that blow? Mr Rowe said death might have arisen from incipient congestion of the brain, caused by a history of ill-usage, culminating in the fall which had produced the external appearances on the skull.

The judge said there was no definite proof of the injury having been inflicted by both of the prisoners, or by one more than the other. He then addressed the jury on the case which 'had involved a most serious and painful enquiry'. According to medical evidence, the cause of death was pressure of blood on the brain, which he attributed to the injury on the back of the head, caused either by a blow or a fall. Had it resulted from a kick or blow by either of the prisoners, that would have been murder or manslaughter, but even then there was nothing to show who had administered the blow. They might suspect that one or other of the prisoners was responsible, but although each one had chastised the girl at various times, it was impossible to apportion blame on one or the other. Much as he deplored saying so, 'the case was of necessity left in that state of uncertainty' and he was bound to tell them that the case for the prosecution had failed. If death had been brought about by privation, or want of food, the male prisoner alone would be held responsible. Had it been a succession of injuries, there would have been a case for convicting both, but it seemed to him that there was nothing on which they could safely convict. The jury therefore returned a verdict of not guilty.

Robert and Sarah Bird were set free – but not for long. In the summer assizes, the case was brought again and they were charged with intent to injure Maria, and with intent by injury to do her grievous bodily harm. They pleaded *autrefois acquit* (previously acquitted), as they had been tried for the same offence at the previous assizes and acquitted. By the law of England no person could be tried twice for the same offence, so the learned commissioner who tried them directed that a verdict should be entered against them. The matter was considered by the Law Lords, and they were called up at Exeter again on 19 March 1851, when Baron Martin passed sentence of imprisonment on Mr and Mrs Bird with hard labour for sixteen months – in effect a sentence of two years from the trial in July 1850.

13

'SHE SHOULD BREAK OFF ALL CORRESPONDENCE WITH ME'

Lynton, 1857

John Barwick was a labourer who lived at Lynton, while Maria Blackmore was a servant at the Valley of Rocks Hotel. They had been going out together for a while, but she disapproved of his heavy drinking. On 16 December 1857, Barwick had spent much of the day drinking at the Globe Inn nearby, and got into a fight with another patron, Mr Lethaby. In the evening he went to his parents' house, sat by the fire, and fell asleep. Meanwhile Maria Blackmore said she wanted to see him and give him a piece of her mind. Her friend, Hannah Mogridge, went to look for him to tell him that Maria needed to speak to him. Barwick was awoken and went into the street when Blackmore joined him.

'You have been drinking today?' Maria asked him. He denied having done so, but when she told him that someone had informed her he had, he admitted it. Hannah Mogridge then went to get some milk, and returned to where the couple were standing. She asked Maria to go back with her. 'Not for a few minutes,' the latter told her, so Hannah left on her own.

Maria and Barwick were seen walking and talking together that evening by various people, some of whom noticed that he had his arm around her neck. Just before ten o'clock a scream was heard. Maria Blackmore later turned up at her friend Mrs Bromham's home and begged her to let her stay for a while. The latter was horrified to see the girl covered in blood, and was about to ask her what had happened when Maria collapsed on the floor. Before medical aid could be summoned, she was dead. A surgeon, John Clark, was called. He found that Maria had been stabbed in the throat, and the jugular vein and common carotid artery had been completely severed.

Lynton.

Barwick was at his house reading the Holy Bible when he was apprehended. When he was searched, a razor and two knives, one covered with blood, were found in his pocket, and there were spots of blood on his hand. As he was taken into custody, he admitted that he had attacked Maria, telling Constable Woodrow, 'She told me that she should break off all correspondence with me that night, and that caused it.' He continued, 'If you had not come when you did, you would not have found me alive.' From this, it was apparent that he had considered killing his sweetheart and then himself.

At the inquest at Lynton the next day, Hannah Mogridge told the court what had happened, while John Clark described the fatal injuries, and Constable Woodrow spoke of the conversation that had followed when he apprehended Barwick. A verdict of wilful murder was returned, and the young man was committed for trial.

Barwick appeared at Exeter Assizes on 16 March 1858 before Mr Justice Willes, with John Karslake and Mr Buller appearing for the prosecution, and Mr John Duke Coleridge for the defence. After evidence on the crime was given, Coleridge summed up in a speech which contended that the act had been perpetrated under a fit of jealousy, and was in no way premeditated.

The jury returned a verdict of guilty, and Barwick was sentenced to be hanged. Meanwhile, magistrates and other senior officials throughout Devon were lobbying the Secretary of State for the sentence to be commuted. Among them was Sir Edward Marwood Elton, the High Sheriff of Devon, who wrote to the Home Secretary:

John Duke Coleridge, Baron Coleridge and later Lord Chief Justice. (© Nicola Sly)

In the course of my official duties as Sheriff I was in attendance in the court during the trial of the miserable culprit, John Barwick, and I paid the greatest attention to the case. In my own mind no doubt exists upon the propriety of the sentence, and that a more righteous judge never presided upon the bench.

I do not advocate by any means the abolition of capital punishment. 'Mercy to the guilty is cruelty to the innocent;' yet before this terrible measure of punishment is inflicted upon the unhappy youth I trust I may be permitted to hope for a further consideration of the sentence.

The fatal act was committed without premeditation: passion, acting upon a weak mind, induced him to use a deadly instrument, which, as it appeared in evidence, falling upon any other part of the body than the jugular vein and common carotid artery, would not have produced much mischief.

I consider this to be a case to which the Royal clemency might not improperly be extended, and I wish my name to be added to the prayer of the petitioners, so that the alteration of the sentence to penal servitude for life might be made to satisfy the ends of justice.

On 13 April the prison chaplain told Barwick that he was due to be executed three days later. He was writing to his mother at the time, and was advised to tell her that this would be the last letter she would ever receive from him. By this time he was resigned to his fate. However, on the following day the prison governor received a letter from the Home Office, advising him that the sentence was commuted to penal servitude for life.

14

'YOU ARE THE CAUSE OF IT'

Plymouth, 1861

During the nineteenth century, there were several murders in military establishments. Boredom, ready access to alcohol, and grievances among soldiers against their superiors were generally the reason, and a combination of all these factors proved fatal all too often. One such case in Devon concerned Henry Jones, of the 61st Regiment quartered at Millbay Barracks, Plymouth. Born in Dover, he joined the army in 1851 at the age of twenty-three, proved an able soldier, and was promoted to the rank of lance-sergeant. A few years later he was stationed at Plymouth.

Robert Hackett, a native of Queen's County (Leinster), Ireland, aged twenty-nine, had served in the army for about ten years. This included a period in India as a soldier at the siege and capture of Delhi, as a result of which he had been awarded a medal and a good conduct stripe. A few years later he found himself in the regiment at Plymouth. On Friday, 5 January 1861, he was paid his wages by Lieutenant Hamilton, and promptly went out for a night on the town. Next day he went to a public house near the barracks where he ordered a quart of whisky, a half gallon of ale, and subsequently a further pint of whisky, which he shared with some of his friends.

At around lunchtime he was in the barrack room where he had a visit from Mr Purcell, an old military pensioner, fellow Irishman, and regular caller at the barracks. Purcell had a long conversation with Hackett about the division of some prize money taken at Delhi, and Hackett gave him a bowl of soup. Jones, who was present, laughed at Purcell's story and said to Hackett, 'Go along you fool, he is spinning that "cuffer" to you to get your dinner.' Purcell commented, 'You can't make a course out of me, I am too old a soldier,' but Jones's remarks were deeply resented by Hackett.

*The walls of Millbay
Barracks. (© Derek Tait)*

Throughout the afternoon Hackett continued to drink, though opinions of those around him later varied as to what state he was in. It is fair, however, to assume that after two or three hours he had consumed more than was good for him, especially as he had presumably gone without any lunch. In the evening, when Purcell had gone and the men were having their tea, he went to the officers' servants' private room, and there loaded his rifle. Returning to the barrack room, he remarked to Jones that he was thankful to 'No 3 and 4 mess for insulting my friend at dinner'.

'What was said to the pensioner was no harm,' Jones answered.

'Harry, you are the cause of it,' was Hackett's rejoinder.

Some increasingly short-tempered exchanges followed, with Hackett telling Jones that he was only a sergeant, and that if it had not been for the threat of receiving fifty lashes he would strike him, as he deeply resented the insult made to his fellow countryman.

Hackett then walked out angrily. About fifteen minutes later he came back with a rifle. Holding the weapon to his hip, he ordered the other men to stand clear. Corporal Ryan, one of the officers present, called out to his colleagues, 'Throw up his rifle,' but before anybody had a chance to intervene, Hackett aimed the rifle and fired at Jones, who was in the next room, about 20 feet away. The latter was standing talking about the orders he had just brought to Colour Sergeant Allen, his back towards Hackett. The bullet hit him and passed through the vertebrae of the spinal column, out through the epigastric region, and struck against the opposite wall. He staggered, fell to the ground, and died instantaneously.

Hackett made no attempt to escape as several men asked him to give up his rifle, which he did willingly, and led him from the barracks to the police cells. When there, he said he did not mean to shoot Jones, but someone else.

An inquest into Jones's death was held on Monday 7 January. Meanwhile Hackett was examined before the magistrates and remanded in custody, charged with murder. He went on trial at Exeter Assizes on 12 March before Mr Justice Willes, with Mr Cox and Mr Lopes prosecuting, and Mr Cole for the defence.

Several witnesses described the events of that fatal day. They could not agree among themselves how drunk Hackett had been at the time. One said he was 'excited but perfectly rational', while another said that when he went back to the barracks in the evening with his rifle he was 'staggering drunk'. Nevertheless Major Deacon, one of the senior officers on duty at the time, testified to Hackett's statement, that he did not intend to kill Sergeant Jones. He believed that the prisoner 'appeared at that time not to be drunk, but to have been drinking for some days'.

Mr Cole then addressed the jury on behalf of the prisoner, saying that this was one of the most distressing cases that had ever been brought before a jury. Here was a young man against whom nobody could say a bad word, charged with the murder of one of his comrades with whom he had been through a very difficult campaign in India, fighting side-by-side against the enemy, on the best of terms with each other, almost like brothers. The only thing he could dispute was whether the prisoner was in a responsible state of mind at the time. For some days he had been drinking heavily, and 'had taken that into his stomach which had stolen away his brains'.

Mr Justice Willes. (© Nicola Sly)

He had come into the mess room with a pensioner and had given him his dinner, which he himself could not eat. When the conversation took a turn about prize money, some jocular observations were made, which would not normally have given offence to anyone. After the prisoner and his friend had left the room they went to have more to drink, before returning at about 5.30 for the exchange which resulted in death.

Hackett accused those in the mess of having insulted his friend, when Jones took it up and said no harm had been intended. Hackett told him that it was his fault, and Jones replied in an offensive tone. Hackett said that if it was not for a threat of fifty lashes, he would 'smash' him. If he dreaded receiving fifty lashes for insubordination, would he have harboured the intention of deliberately killing his old comrade? And why had the prosecution not proved what the prisoner had done in his absence from the mess room? Where was the evidence to show that the prisoner had loaded the rifle, or that he knew it was loaded? The man's life was at stake, and why had the prosecution not made every inquiry?

The disparity in some of the witnesses' evidence was also emphasised. One had described the prisoner as 'staggering drunk', and another said he was sober. It had been the former man's duty to take him into custody if he was drunk, but the man had neglected his duty. He had not gone before the magistrates and given any evidence at the time; only now had he come to give any evidence, and much of it did not ring true. It was apparent that the prisoner was in a state of absolute delerium after having been drinking for several days, and had fired off a rifle which he did not realise was loaded. He had stated that he never intended to shoot his old comrade Sergeant Jones.

The prisoner and Jones were in two different rooms at the time, and it was sheer chance that the bullet went through the doorway. If a man was 'staggering drunk', he could hardly have aimed at Jones in the other room, eleven yards away, so as to strike him, and take his life. It must surely have been an accident. In a case of murder there must be a deliberate intention formed in a man's mind. Was this man in such a state as to know what he was about? Did he know the rifle was loaded, and did he intentionally discharge it? The result of the jury's verdict, if guilty, would be the death of the unfortunate man before them. If they made a mistake, and the man went to his death, such an error could never be rectified. If they had any doubt, they were bound to give the prisoner the benefit of it.

In summing up, Mr Justice Willes said there was no doubt that Jones had been killed by the bullet. If murder was causing the death of another either through direct malice or from that malice which the law implied, no provocation by word could palliate the offence or reduce the offence from murder to manslaughter. Unless a man's drunkenness had produced a morbid state of mind, it would not excuse him, and 'mere drunkenness would not suffice'. There was no evidence of any such state of mind in this case. Every man was presumed to be answerable for his act unless he was in such a state of mind that he was perfectly unconscious of any act he did, but it would be for them to say whether they could come to such a result in this case. If the evidence

Executioner William Calcraft.

satisfied them that the prisoner discharged his rifle intentionally at the sergeant, it would be their duty to find him guilty of murder.

The jury retired at 3.50 p.m., and took half an hour to return with a verdict of guilty, adding that the prisoner should be recommended to mercy. The judge then passed a sentence of death on him, adding that there was little chance that mercy would be extended to him on this side of the grave.

On 30 March, just under three weeks later, Hackett kept his date with the gallows. Early in the morning the Revd James Eccles, a Roman Catholic priest, visited him in his cell and remained with him until the moment came for him to be led out. In his final words to the priest, Hackett maintained that he did not intend to shoot Sergeant Jones, and blamed it all on drink. He was hanged by William Calcraft.

15

'I DID NOT KNOW WHAT TO DO'

Plymouth, 1866

In the 1860s a series of fortifications were built along the south coast. Seven-year-old Philip Boobier was the son of a labourer employed to help build the walls at Staddon Fort, Jennycliff, on the coast at Plymouth. He was an exceptionally intelligent lad, who enjoyed playing there, and was much liked by the soldiers, especially those of the 13th Regiment quartered near the town. At about 8 p.m. on the evening of Saturday, 9 June 1866, he left home, taking with him a book to read to Sergeant Parsons, an officer who had become a particularly good friend and was helping him with his reading.

Half an hour later the boy was seen going to the camp with Private John Grant, who belonged to Parsons's mess and tent, and then afterwards going to a place where the soldiers were playing at pitch and toss. Grant, a 35-year-old Irishman, was known in the regiment as an accomplished wrestler and boxer. His colleagues neither liked nor trusted him. He had already been under arrest several times for military offences, including insubordination to his seniors, and, previous to enlisting

Staddon Heights, 1971. (© Steve Johnson)

in the army, it was understood he had been charged with what was discreetly referred to in the press as 'the commission of an unnatural offence'.

About half an hour later, the prisoner was seen by a Mr Atkins returning, but without the child. He appeared rather excited as he walked over to Atkins, and asked him if there was any Dublin man who could fight or wrestle. Soon afterwards he was seen climbing over a hedge, and it was noticed that he had blood on his cheek, hand and trousers.

At about four o'clock the next morning, Grant was seen coming from the rear of the officers' tents. Matilda Boobier, who had been looking for her son all night, followed him in to his tent, asking him where he had left Philip. He said rather rudely that he had never seen the boy. Shortly after that her husband, Philip, also came and asked Grant the same question, and again Grant denied any knowledge of the child. Mr Boobier then asked him where he had been all night, and Grant said he had been at a public house. He was then taken to a guardroom, where he continued to deny any knowledge of the child. After a while he changed his mind and admitted that the boy had come with him to wash, but he was so drunk that he could not tell what had become of him.

At midday on Sunday, the boy's body was found under a furze bush in a ditch, close to the direction in which he and Grant had been seen going the previous evening. A post-mortem examination was carried out by Mr Wilson, a surgeon, who found marks of severe contusions on the face, neck and chest, and the tongue protruding. He was sure such wounds could not have been caused by a fall or an accident, but must have been inflicted by some blunt instrument and repeated blows. No single blow could have caused the injuries. Grant was apprehended and held in custody.

Grant called Sergeant Hicks to the cell, and said he wanted to be taken before a magistrate. When told that this wish could not be granted, after being cautioned, he made a statement:

On the Saturday evening I was going down to bathe. I went across the ball-firing ground, and was told there were rabbits, and I took up a stone and flung it at a rabbit, but accidentally struck the boy instead of the rabbit. The boy fell from place to place. I went to him and lifted him up, and put him on my knee for ten minutes. He then asked me to put him down, and I did so. He did not appear to be much hurt. I was going to lift him up again, but he said 'no'. I went to the camp. I then returned, and remained with him till 3 o'clock, when he died. I did not know what to do; but I returned to the camp.

When a search was made of the spot where the body was found, a stick was discovered, concealed under the long grass.

Grant appeared at Exeter Assizes on 27 July before Mr Justice Blackburn, with Mr Lopes and Mr Clark for the prosecution, and Mr Bere for the defence.

At the trial, the first witness for the prosecution was Sergeant Noah Nicks. He produced a plan which he had made partly from an ordnance sheet and partly from an actual survey, showing the place where he believed the murder was committed. Mr Bere objected to the map, and the judge therefore ruled that it could not be used.

Thomas Atkins, a bugler in the 13th Regiment of foot, stationed at Staddon Heights at that time, said the prisoner had been in that regiment, and had been there about a week. He saw Grant coming from his tent, wearing a greatcoat, with a stick in one hand and a towel in the other. He watched the soldier and the boy playing together for a while at the washing ground. Several other soldiers gave similar evidence.

The prosecution maintained that Grant had left the camp with Philip, took him to the ditch, and killed him. He returned to the camp, but realising that he had left the body exposed, went back and put it in a more secret spot. Grant had admitted in his statement that he caused the child's death, and the only question was whether the jury believed the death had been caused by a wilful or accidental act by the prisoner.

In addressing the jury on behalf of the prisoner, Mr Bere said that there had been no motive for him to attack the deceased. After the judge had summed up, the jury retired for an hour and returned a verdict of guilty. During the next two weeks Grant was regularly visited by the Catholic priest at Exeter, and Dr Vaughan, Bishop of Plymouth. He was hanged on 15 August – the last public execution at Exeter.

16

'GOT INTO TROUBLE'

Roborough, 1870

In the autumn of 1869, Mary Ann Trewin, a servant aged about 21 who worked for a farming family in the Yelverton area, realised that she was expecting a child. As was so often the case in those days, she was probably a good-natured but naive girl who had been seduced by a young male servant, 'got into trouble', and was discharged. On 21 December she was admitted to the Tavistock Union Workhouse, and on 16 April 1870 she gave birth to a daughter.

One month later, on 18 May, she discharged herself. When Maria Palmer, the workhouse nurse, asked where she was intending to go, Mary said she was going to see friends at Buckland Monachorum, near Yelverton, who would be able to care for the child. After that she intended to return to her previous employers.

A little later John Giles, a Bickleigh farmer, was driving his sheep over Roborough Downs when he recognised Mary walking along the turnpike road from Tavistock, carrying a babe in arms. She was making her way from the workhouse.

The former Tavistock Union Workhouse, now Russell Court, a development of residential flats.
(© Trevor James)

Sensing that something was not quite right, he watched her turn off the highway into a lane leading to the hamlet at Clearbrook. Shortly afterwards she arrived at the house of her friend Ann Arfon, who asked about the baby. Mary told her sorrowfully that the little one had died and been buried the previous Saturday.

Two days later, Samuel Luscombe, a water bailiff, was at Devonport Leat, which crossed Roborough Down nearby. He found the body of a baby lying on the bank, covered the little figure with furze and went to the police station at Roborough to report the find. He must have made enquiries beforehand, finding out where the child had come from and who the mother was, as he then went to the Skylark Inn, Clearbrook, to ask after Miss Trewin. By this time she was staying at the home of Mr and Mrs Lillicrap, where she had lived for a short time before going to the Union Workhouse.

When she was questioned by Sergeant Butt, Mary repeated her story that the baby had died in the workhouse and been buried. The policeman then challenged her as to what her answer would be if he contacted the Master to enquire whether a child had died there and been buried, as she claimed. When she made no reply, she was taken into custody and charged with the murder of her baby daughter.

On 24 May, an inquest was held at Roborough Police Court before Mr W.C. Radcliffe. Mr Willis, the surgeon who had performed the post-mortem examination, said that in his opinion death was due to drowning. Maria Palmer, from the workhouse, confirmed details of Mary Trewin's six-month stay there and identified the baby as being Miss Trewin's child. She added that when Mary had left Tavistock, her baby was in perfect health.

The Skylark Inn, Clearbrook. (© Paul Rendell)

Roborough police station. (© Simon Dell)

After the coroner had summed up, the jury returned a verdict of wilful murder against Mary. The next day she was formally charged with murder and committed for trial at the next Assizes, saying nothing in her defence.

On 28 July she was tried at Exeter Assizes for murdering her child before Mr Justice Willes, with Mr Clark prosecuting and nobody to defend her. The main witness for the prosecution was Mr Willis, who said that he had examined the prisoner and considered she was mentally defective, although she knew right from wrong. Other witnesses called, including Mrs Palmer, gave similar testimony, saying that Mary seemed to be rather 'soft'. At no stage did Mary say anything in her defence or give any sign of wishing to, and she looked throughout as if she was taking no interest in the proceedings.

No witnesses were called for the defence, and the evidence was purely circumstantial. In summing up, the judge told the jury that if Mary had killed her child in malice, or put her into the water intentionally, she was guilty of murder. They had to consider the evidence and decide that if the child had got into the water as a result of culpable negligence, and Mary had therefore brought about her death by carelessness, without malice, the crime was one of manslaughter. Was she responsible for her actions? It was clear that she was guilty of either the greater or the lesser offence, and the question for them was whether she was such a person as in law who was answerable for her actions. In his judgement there was no evidence

Tavistock.

Tavistock Guildhall, police station and court gate archway, late nineteenth century. (© Simon Dell)

upon which she could be acquitted on that ground. The law required much more evidence than that which had been put forward in court with regard to aberration of mind to justify an acquittal on the grounds of insanity.

The jury returned a verdict of manslaughter. In sentencing Mary, the judge told her that she had stood in great peril of being committed on the graver charge. He would not be doing his duty if he did not pass on her a sentence which to a girl like her might appear very heavy, and which might at the same time act as a warning to others. Lest any other woman disposed to disregard her children and endanger their lives take warning, for if she had not been a girl whose wits were weak, the jury would have given a more serious verdict. He sentenced her to seven years' penal servitude.

17

'I NEVER HURTED THE POOR MAN'

James Pepperell of Lyme Regis, aged about 30, was a farm labourer, noted for being particularly skilled and thus able to command good wages. Much of his money went on drink, and he was apt to boast rather unwisely that he never travelled without enough money to pay his expenses. On 22 April 1870 he left his lodgings at Membury, three miles from Axminster, and went to the steeplechasing at Colyton. That evening he went to the White Hart Inn, where he was joined by Miss Sutton and James Harris, both acquaintances of his from Lyme Regis. They had a few drinks together and stayed until the village constable came in at about eleven o'clock and asked everyone to drink up and leave. Pepperell paid the bar bill just before they left separately, within a few minutes of each other. Harris was perfectly sober, but the other two were rather the worse for wear.

That was the last anybody saw of Pepperell for almost three weeks. Nobody was concerned at first, as he had frequently taken himself off at times and disappeared for a few days. However, this time he never returned. On 10 May a police officer was crossing a bridge over the River Axe, when he saw something floating in the water. When it was brought out onto the bank, it was identified as the body of Pepperell. His face, head and neck had been attacked with a stick. After making enquiries, suspicion immediately fell on Harris, who had been seen carrying a stick when he was at Colyton. He denied having anything to do with the attack on Pepperell, and asked his wife to swear that he had been asleep at home all evening. This did him no good at all, as there were several witnesses who were equally prepared to testify that he had been at the White Hart Inn that evening. Spots of blood were found on his coat, which he insisted were from a rabbit he had killed. Nevertheless, he was arrested and charged with murder.

An inquest was held at the White Hart Inn. The first witness called was Elizabeth Boyting, who said Pepperell had been lodging in her house on a regular basis for the last few years. Joshua Richards, who had been in the inn on the night of the races, had heard Harris's footsteps going as far as the railway station towards Axbridge, before they stopped suddenly. When Pepperell left about ten minutes later, he went in the same direction and Miss Sutton went the other way, towards Colyton. Richards then went across the fields and saw her near Holy Cross Gate, a few minutes after she had left the inn. She was with a policeman, Constable Walters, who was walking her back home part of the way for her own safety as she was so drunk, and needed to know the way to Colyton. It was the last Richards saw of her than evening.

Simon Fowler, a farmer, who lived near Axbridge, said that on the morning after the races he saw Harris emerging from his cowshed, and spoke to him angrily. The latter said he had been to the races the previous day and was sleeping it off. Once he was back on the road, he seemed uncertain which direction to take. Fowler added that he went to bed about twenty minutes to midnight on the night of the races, and he remembered hearing cries coming from the direction of Axbridge. They sounded like that of a man in distress, and were at first rather loud. After hearing them three times, he remarked to his wife that there was 'someone halloaing pretty well on Axbridge,' and she told him that it would be people returning from the races. While they were speaking he heard the sound another three or four times, but in a lower tone. If it had been any other night, he would have taken more notice of it, but he assumed it was just people returning from the races. He thought some parties had been fighting, and one of them had got the worst of it and was crying for help or mercy, or something of the kind. There were two other people in his house who also heard the cries.

John Pepperell, father of the deceased, said he had been to the house where his son was lodging. He found his working and other clothes there as well as his tools, but no money or any other possessions. His son never told him how much money he earned, and did not know whether he had saved any, but he always had plenty of money when he came to see him, often with gold among it.

George Hore, a miller of Lexhayne Mills, Shute, said that on the morning after the races he saw a man who told him his name was Harris, and he was probably the prisoner now present. He was lying on the bank of a field on Crabhayne Farm, and when Hore saw him he said, 'Well, my friend, you have had a bit of a nap.'

'Yes I have; I am very cold,' Harris replied. Hore asked him if he had been to the races, and he confirmed that he had. 'I suppose you took a little drop too much?'

'Yes I have,' said Harris, 'and now I am very dry.'

After some more conversation, Hore asked him how he came to be there. Harris said he did not know, and did not even know where he was.

'If you'll be advised by me,' said Hore firmly, 'you'll be moving, and then you will be much better than if you lie here.'

Harris repeated that he was very dry, and, taking pity on him, Hore offered to buy him a drink at the White Hart, about half a mile away. At first Harris was reluctant to accept the hospitality, saying, 'I don't know about going with you,' and then added, 'I'll take off this slop, or they'll say I am a rough looking fellow.' Then he said he had a wife and three or four children at Lyme Regis. They went together to the White Hart, and as Harris was passing Axbridge he looked over on the south side. At the inn Hore gave him a pint of ale and he sat by the fire drinking, complaining that he was very cold. Hore left him behind at the inn.

When cross-examined, Harris said he had seen a stick lying on the ground beside him. He said he had also told Hore he intended to look for work.

Emma Quick, wife of the landlord of the White Hart, recalled having seen Harris and Miss Sutton there on the night of the races, both drinking with Pepperell. It had been shortly before ten o'clock, and she remembered Miss Sutton had been there for over an hour already, while Harris was resting on his stick. Pepperell paid for all the drinks, and Miss Sutton was definitely the worse for wear, although she was not aware that any of them had been quarrelling or creating a disturbance. At eleven o'clock she called a policeman to clear the premises, but by then only George Hooper, William Hazell, Harris, Pepperell and Constable Gunn were still left. About ten minutes later Harris left in the direction of Axbridge, though she did not see how far he went. Pepperell, Miss Sutton and the policeman left about ten minutes later, Pepperell towards Axebridge and the other two towards Colyford. Next morning she saw Harris at about eleven o'clock with Hore, and they had some conversation during which he remarked that he had not been home, 'I laid down over here,' he said, although he did not say exactly where. She told him he must have had 'a rough bed', and he agreed.

William Hazell, a platelayer on the railway, said he noticed Harris and Pepperell in the White Hart on the race night, and they were still there when he left, with Miss Sutton sitting between them. He remembered Harris having a stick, and also his telling them that he had to go to Lyme that night. Several other witnesses spoke of seeing Harris and Pepperell either at the races or the public house that day.

Finally, two police officers took the stand. Constable Gunn said that on the morning of 6 May he saw Harris at Colyford, charged him with wilful murder, and gave him the usual caution, to which he replied, 'It isn't me that done it, sir.' When he pointed out to Harris the spots of blood on his clothes, the latter insisted it was rabbit's blood. On 8 May he went to Lyme Regis and searched Harris's house, where he found a shirt with spots of blood on the left sleeve, which he produced in court. Police-Superintendent Dore added that the blood was dry and had probably been there some time. When cross-examined, Harris angrily said, 'I never hurted the poor man and I'm innocent.'

Nobody could be certain whether the blood was human or animal. Dr Taylor said that the blood of birds and fishes was easily distinguishable from that of man, but there was difficulty in distinguishing that of man from rabbits, dogs and hares, and the problem was exacerbated with dried blood on clothing, which was almost impossible to tell apart, so there was no point in sending it away for analysis. As for several of the witnesses mentioning Harris having a stick with him at Colyton and his fervent denial that he had one at all, it was for the jury to draw their own conclusions – it was his word against theirs. It was fair for Harris to say there did not

A group of Devon policemen, 1871. (© Simon Dell)

appear to be any ill-feeling between him and Pepperell, and there was no evidence to show that he knew in which direction Pepperell had been going, or that he knew Pepperell had any money in his possession.

Harris had clearly not been telling the truth, firstly about getting home at 2 a.m. after the races, and secondly about the stick. While it was always suspicious when a man told such lies, the coroner said that he did not think it was altogether conclusive, as a man who found himself in trouble would often be foolish enough to tell lies to get rid of matters which seemed against him. It was extraordinary that he did not go home on the night in question, or the next morning, and also remarkable that he should return to the White Hart, where he had been drinking the previous night. If he was guilty of the crime, it was, to say the least, rather odd of him to return to the inn.

The jury were out for quarter of an hour, and returned with a verdict of wilful murder. After hearing the verdict Harris seemed stunned, but continued to protest his innocence.

The case was among those due to come before the Exeter Assizes that summer. However, on 28 July 1870, the Grand Jury threw out the indictment against Harris, claiming that there was insufficient evidence to place before the magistrates. For the prosecution, Mr Collins told the court that as this had been done, he therefore did not propose to offer any evidence. Mr Justice Willes then directed the jury to acquit the prisoner. Nobody would ever be brought to justice for the death of James Pepperell.

18

'THEY WANT TO PUT ME AWAY'

Plymouth, 1874

In 1868 Sylvanus Sweet, a tanner, married Elizabeth Ann Watts, daughter of Isaac Watts, proprietor of the Globe Hotel, Bedford Street, in Plymouth. They settled in a house at Clifton Place, and lived together for about a year. The marriage proved an unhappy one, made worse by Sylvanus's regular epileptic fits. The couple separated and began divorce proceedings while Elizabeth went back her family home, but the divorce was never finalised, and husband and wife were later reconciled.

For a few months, they appeared to be perfectly happy, but it all went badly wrong on 28 January 1874, a day on which they had arranged to go out for tea. Sylvanus said he was going to put some pomatum (hair tonic) on his head, and Elizabeth told him it was 'nasty stuff', suggesting he should use oil instead. They went upstairs together, and a couple of minutes later Sylvanus came down to send the servant girl out for some pomatum. While she was away, the neighbours heard screams coming from the house. Sylvanus then ran out looking very excited, and went to the Guildhall, where he complained that his father-in-law, his wife, and Sir Edward Bates, the local Conservative Member of Parliament who had just been canvassing him for his vote in the forthcoming general election, were intending to send him to an asylum.

When the servant returned to the house, she went to the bedroom, and found her mistress lying on the floor covered with blood. Beside her lay a cutlass, clotted with blood. In the heat of the moment Sylvanus had taken the cutlass hanging on the wall, and struck Elizabeth repeatedly across the head and on the hand, which she had raised to try and protect herself. He then rained blows on her prostrate body. She lay moaning on the floor and died from her injuries about twenty minutes later.

Meanwhile, Sylvanus had gone to the nearest police station. On arrival he behaved very oddly, and two doctors were called to examine him. The first said he thought the man was insane and unaccountable for his actions, while the second said he was merely shamming.

Plymouth Guildhall.

On 29 January, Sylvanus was brought before the magistrates and charged with murdering his wife. The servant was called as a witness, and said that husband and wife had been on the best of terms until they had the argument.

He went on trial before Mr Justice Quinn at Exeter Assizes on 14 March, with Mr Cole and Mr McKellar prosecuting, Mr Lopes and Mr Charles defending. Sylvanus Sweet, the reporters noted, 'appeared greatly distressed' as counsel gave details of the killing.

For the prosecution, Mr Cole said that the only possible defence that could be given was that the prisoner was in a state of mind which rendered him not responsible for his actions. He could not see anything in the case which would enable them to reduce the crime to manslaughter. Proceedings were then interrupted when a juryman was taken ill and a fresh jury was empanelled. After resuming, Mr Cole went on to say that if a defence of insanity was set up, it was his duty to see that it was proved.

Isaac Watts, Elizabeth's father, said that after the couple had terminated their divorce proceedings and got back together again he thought they were perfectly happy. On the day of the murder, he had called at their house with Sir Edward Bates and John Hammett, a painter, who were both on a canvassing expedition. They all had some conversation together, and Sylvanus remarked that he would like to have something to do, presumably to help. Watts suggested that he ought to go to the committee room and get a book. He only stayed for a few minutes, and left about three o'clock. At the time he did not notice anything strange about his son-in-law's

Bedford Street, Plymouth. (© Derek Tait)

*A Plymouth Borough policeman,
c. 1870. (© Simon Dell)*

manner. Despite the prisoner's assertions, nothing had been said about threatening to send him to an asylum. His health seemed perfectly good.

On being cross-examined, Mr Watts said he was aware that Sylvanus was subject to epileptic fits, and had known since shortly after the marriage, and that he knew they had continued since.

Mr Hammett confirmed that he had been to the house with Sir Edward Bates on the day of the killing, and said he had noticed something 'unfavourable' at the time about the look of the prisoner. When cross-examined, he said there seemed to be 'a reserve and absence about him' – he thought he had a strange look, and felt he was 'not in his right mind'.

Emily Donovan, the servant, said that she had been employed by Sylvanus at the beginning of January, and that the Sweets kept their bedroom door unlocked in the daytime and locked at night. As far as she was aware they lived very comfortably together, and she had never observed anything peculiar in Sylvanus's manner. He always treated his wife with affection and kindness, and seemed generally cheerful. On the 27th he appeared perfectly normal. They took their meals as usual that day, and after dinner Mrs Sweet went to do some ironing in the front parlour. Her husband was there part of the time, and they were talking about going to Stoke for tea. He went upstairs, then came down and asked her for her keys. She was folding some clothes and when he asked her if she was going to iron them, she said no.

He then said he wished he had some pomade. 'You shan't have any of the stinking stuff,' she retorted. 'You shan't come near me if you do.'

A group of
Plymouth Borough
policemen,
c. 1870.
(© Simon Dell)

The couple went upstairs together, and after a while he came down to ask Miss Donovan to go to Sanders' on Mutley Plain for a shilling bottle of the substance. Emily went out, and was gone about quarter of an hour. When she came back she saw two women at the door, and also noticed Emilia Doidge at her front door opposite. On going upstairs she found the bedroom door open, and saw Mrs Sweet lying on her back with her head to the door, covered in blood. She went for a policeman, and when she came back to the house she found one there talking to the doctors.

Mrs Doidge, who lived opposite, said she had heard three very loud screams, and probably blows as well, from the Sweets' bedroom. Immediately afterwards she saw Mr Sweet coming out of the front door, wearing his hat and putting on his greatcoat. As he walked out he looked 'very hurried, white, and very excited'. After he passed her he ran down the street, and about four minutes later she saw Miss Donovan coming back. It had been a tremendous shock to her, as she too thought that husband and wife had always seemed very happy together.

John Yabsley, of Woodland Place, said he was passing Clifton Place that afternoon. After being told what had happened, he went into the house and into the Sweets' bedroom, saw Mrs Sweet lying on her side, with a sword lying nearby. He placed his hand gently on her and she groaned. Blood was oozing from her head and face, which were badly cut, and he took a towel to try and staunch the flow. He had known Elizabeth since childhood, but he would not have known it was her if he had not been aware that she lived there. On cross-examination, he said that she appeared to have been struck repeatedly.

Constable William Venton went to the Sweets' house that afternoon and found Elizabeth's body lying on the floor. He went for a doctor and came back with Mr Square, who found a sword which he produced, with a square blade about 2 feet long, covered with blood. Then he went to the Guildhall, found Sweet there, lying on his back in the police station, and asked him to get up.

'Hallo, Venton, you are the best friend I have got,' Sweet said to him brokenly. He repeated between sobs that his wife, Mr Watts and Mr Bates were all trying to send him to an asylum. His wife was always wanting money, and he had just agreed to pay her £50 a year, yet she was still not satisfied. On cross-examination, Venton said that Sweet was terribly excited, and demanding to see a doctor. The fear of being sent to an asylum weighed particularly on his mind.

Henry Dulling, a cab driver, said Sweet came to him that afternoon and told him to drive to the Guildhall as quickly as possible. He observed nothing peculiar. He drove to the Guildhall, where Sweet got out and ran up the steps. As he got out of the cab his hat fell off, but he did not stop to retrieve it. He told Dulling to get a policeman and the latter called Inspector Murch. He offered Sweet his hat, but he would not take it. When he got out of the cab he definitely seemed 'strange'.

Mr Eccles, the surgeon, went to the Sweets' house on the afternoon of the murder, went to the front bedroom, and found Mrs Sweet on the floor, insensible and with no discernible pulse. She had about ten wounds on her skull, each one fracturing the bone, as well as severe wounds on her arms and hands. There were splashes of blood

on the ceiling and walls of the room, and a large
pool of blood on the floor, and her dress was covered
with blood.

When an attack of epilepsy comes on, he said, the
patient usually turns pale. It was also common for them to
suffer stomach pains, delirium and even madness. A person
might become delirious in ten minutes, and when driven to commit
an act, it was generally violent, or termed *epilepticus furore*. From
the nature of the wounds, he believed that Sweet was having an epileptic fit at the
time, and was probably not aware of what he was doing at the time. Such patients
generally suffered from delusions. At the time he attacked his wife he was suffering
from the illness, and he had had another attack in prison the previous Monday. The
evidence was corroborated by a second surgeon in court, William Square, who went
on to say that epileptic patients were often a danger to those around them. 'Sudden
invasion was a character of the disease,' he said. 'It passed off suddenly, and the
patient lost all idea of what he had said or done.'

Inspector Murch, who had seen Sweet at the Guildhall and was unaware of this
medical history, immediately supposed Sweet to have been drunk. He was rambling
about, crying, and muttering that 'they' wanted him put in the asylum. Although he
told Murch to go away, the latter got him downstairs and into the street. He walked
a few yards, then said he would not go home, as 'they want to put me away.' He then
got him to the police station, he lay on the floor, and Murch then realised he was
sober after all. He complained of pains in his stomach and his hand, and his tongue
was dry. He asked to see a doctor, and Dr Stevens, the police surgeon, was sent for.
Murch noticed that Sweet's trousers had blood on them, and his waistcoat was torn,
as if he had been involved in a struggle. When charged with murder, his reaction
was, 'I did not kill my wife. Is she dead?'

Elizabeth Hex, who had been Sweet's housekeeper for two and a half years, said
that she knew he suffered very severe fits during the time she was employed by him.
Before and after he had them, 'he was like a man out of his mind.' He would hurl
things around the house and break them. After they had passed, he did not recall
what had taken place, and denied that he had done anything.

At this stage the judge asked the jury if they thought that the prisoner was
responsible for his actions at the time or not. A juryman asked if these attacks were
hereditary, and a witness, the prisoner's brother, Charles, replied that Sylvanus had
been subject to these attacks for about twelve years, since he was sixteen. They had
an aunt who was subject to similar fits. A juryman said he knew the aunt, and could
vouch that this was correct. The jury believed that the prisoner was insane at the
time of the murder, and the judge ordered him to be confined during Her Majesty's
pleasure.

19

'I AM WILLING TO GO ACCORDING TO JUSTICE'

Plymouth, 1874

Five months after Elizabeth Sweet was battered to death by her husband, the people of Plymouth were horrified by another violent killing which took place in very similar circumstances.

Thomas MacDonald, aged 35, was a former marine who had been discharged from the service on health grounds. He had formed a liaison with Bridget Walsh, the wife of another sailor who spent much of his time away at sea. Mr and Mrs Walsh had two young children, Susanna and Thomas. During the autumn naval manoeuvres of 1873, at which time her husband was absent, Bridget moved in with MacDonald, who lived at the Newcastle Inn, a former public house now let out in tenements, in Fore Street, Stonehouse. Before long they began quarrelling, particularly about money and the ownership of various items of furniture.

Stonehouse in the late nineteenth century.

In the spring of 1874, MacDonald was admitted to the Royal Naval Hospital for about two months. Shortly after he was discharged, he heard from friends and acquaintances that during that time Bridget had been somewhat free with her favours with other men. As he had been living with her while she was still married to somebody else, it was hardly reasonable for him to complain that she had been unfaithful to him. Nevertheless, this so-called infidelity rankled, as did their unresolved arguments about financial matters and furniture.

On the evening of 28 June, Bridget's 14-year-old son Thomas went into one of the rooms to find his mother on the floor. MacDonald had one hand on her throat, as if trying to choke her, and in the other hand he held a poker. She was bleeding at the mouth, and there was blood on the sleeve of her dress. When Thomas appeared MacDonald let go of her, but the quarrelling continued, as he grumbled repeatedly about the furniture. Thomas left the house at half past six, with MacDonald apparently asleep on the sofa.

About three hours later a neighbour, Jane Phillips, called around to visit. Both were in the room together, and Bridget was still very sore from her rough treatment earlier. She showed Jane the marks on her neck, adding that if her son had not arrived when he did, she would surely have been murdered. Jane stayed with them for about two hours, until nearly midnight. As she was leaving, out of MacDonald's hearing, she told Bridget that it was time she left him.

Early next morning MacDonald went to see William White, an innkeeper at Stonehouse. He asked to borrow a shilling, spent it on brandy at a public house, and then returned home. In the afternoon, neighbours became rather concerned after not having seen nor heard anything of either of them for several hours. Fearing the worst, they called White to come and break the door down. When he had forced an entrance, he went inside to see Bridget Welsh lying on the floor in a pool of blood, her head and face battered in. By her side lay MacDonald, unconscious, also bleeding, and at first glance equally lifeless.

Thomas Pearse, a surgeon, was called to the Newcastle Inn about one o'clock and saw two bodies on the floor, apparently dead. The woman had been dead for several hours, as she was cold and stiff. He believed the murder had been committed long before eight o'clock that morning, possibly late the previous night. A handkerchief over her face was soiled with blood, while the skull was broken in two places – over the left temple and on top of the head. The hair was matted and there was much blood on the floor near the head. The man's pulse was even and quiet, the eyes were shut, and on moving him he saw that the throat had been cut. Pearse gave him some water, and he moved his arms and legs a little. When questioned he replied incoherently, repeating the word 'justice' several times and muttering that the woman had been unfaithful to him. There was some vomit by his side, and in the room was some phosphor paste, used for poisoning rats, and a spoon containing traces of a crystallised substance, with a razor lying nearby.

Constable Reep, from Stonehouse police station, found some written documents under a copy of the Testament on the table in the corner of the room, as well as a bank book and a purse containing about £6. Among these items was a letter which read:

Friends and brethren, which I may call all, as we all proceeded from one father and mother. I wanted this woman to go with her husband, and that she would have money in the bank, or all if she liked. I said also in case I found out any other bad works or disabilities that she would suffer the fate that she now undergo. She called me everything but a gentleman, and continued to do so, and for that I ended her days, and for going out with other men. And she would swear that she never lay with any, but I can prove she did, and now for the deed. In tears, I lament the sinful life I spent with her. It is time for to repent and think on eternity. The day is coming fast that we shall all go at last to answer for the past, and think on eternity. Good Christians, will you know how our souls has been exposed in every sinful mode in which we take delight, watching, violating, cursing, and blaspheming, and annoying our neighbours morning, noon and night. Lust and fornication and vile insinuation bring more damnation to our sinful souls, priding in each action of scandal and detraction, and all these sinful actions. I never could control on the holy Sabbath, which God Himself has made. In holy works and prayers, we all that day should join the holy congregations in pious exaltation to the holy elevation of the Sunday service. We all should go. I am true and always true, and never deceived my dear Bridget of a penny but she deceived me in every respect, after me buying nearly all the things in the house. She said I got nothing to do with anything in the house. That was tormenting, and wanted peace as I have now. Let all young women beware, and don't torment men too long, for ye shall surely suffer what my dear Bridget suffered. Me and her shall soon have to go to see the Lord; and I say in this note, before God, that I did not know any other woman but her since I met her, about five years ago, although she may say different. But, still, God have mercy on her soul, and also on my own poor soul, for she and I were always pleasant until a strange party put asunder us both. I hope these writings will be placed after each other. Dr McShane I still remember your disability to me above all other men breathing, and Dr Greening, bigheaded, bigbellied man, confine me to bed; put me on low, and put me in the venereal ward, for fear I would have visitors. And he stopped my visitors. And, as for sticking plaster Jack, I owes him a grudge. Colonel Penrose is the whole cause of this, that would not grant night passes; and he better take care of himself, the villain, that ought to do to others as he wished to be done to. I must end and come to close this note. I can say to the heart she tempted me both night and day, and I believe she and me were born to a bad fate; although I am a man of justice, and nothing but justice for me. Deceived I will not be. If I cannot by fair I will by foul means perform justice. There is £15 odd in the bank. Give it to the poor to pray for her and me, and I will poison myself in case I can get sugar of lead. I am afraid I will be taken before I can end my life. The chest of drawers is for Susanna, and all her mother's clothes. All the furniture to the poor of the town to pray for our souls. Of all those other £6 3s 9½d (the money in the purse) give £2 to the Catholic priest to read masses for me and my dear Bridget, and the remainder to Scott, and also one suit of clothes that he made for me. Give all my other clothes to Mrs Sullivan's husband. I forgive the world, and hope the Lord will forgive me. Never tell any of my relations that ever I was in Plymouth, in case my pension will be given up. Give it to all the pensioners to remember me. Divide fair, and serve all alike. I hope I shall be in heaven along with poor Bridget. God bless both of us.

Alongside it was a shorter letter addressed to his victim. The fact that he was writing to somebody whom he almost certainly knew was already dead may be taken as some indication of either his state of mind or his drunkenness:

My dearly beloved, - You are dead, and I will soon after follow you. In case I was married to you, you would not have lived half so long; but still, I loved you dearly, and always did until you betrayed me on account of other; but you have no other chance. Although I loved you dear, yourself caused me to commit the dreadful deed I have done. In the presence of God, I say I don't know another woman from a man but you since the first night we met. I would take you to Australia or any other part where you would come willingly, but for your connections here close handy, and in the Lord Warden there is proof of other things. I won't mention any absurd matter. If she had trusted those men she would have had but 3s a week and her clothes in pawn, as when I met her. To the grave I am willing to go according to justice. I won't mention any friend or foe. I hope God will forgive them all.

Dr Pearse was called to examine both bodies. He thought that Mrs Walsh had been dead for several hours, but detected a pulse in MacDonald, who was revived. The leg of a bedstead beside them, covered with blood, hair and parts of her brain, had obviously been the weapon. Although he had cut his throat and swallowed poison, he had failed in his aim of suicide. He was admitted once again to the Royal Naval Hospital, where Superintendent Brutton of Stonehouse Police charged him on Monday evening with the murder.

'I must bear it,' MacDonald answered. 'I will tell you, sir, how it was. I lived with her some time. I bought the house and gave her my money. While I was in the hospital she went with other men, and when I came out she would not give me even the price of a pint of porter, and said I had nothing to do with anything in the house.' When asked if he had anything else to say, he admitted that he had killed her, had left some papers and his bank book on the table, and wanted his money to be given to the poor of Stonehouse.

At first he refused to eat, and for several days he was fed by stomach pump until he regained his appetite. He then vowed he would continue to eat heartily until his execution, a fate to which he was resigned. After the inquest on Mrs Walsh he was committed for trial for wilful murder, and once he was judged fit enough to leave hospital he was held in custody at Exeter gaol.

On 25 July he went on trial at Exeter Assizes before Mr Justice Brett, with Mr Lewis prosecuting and Mr Collins defending. When asked how he would plead, he answered 'guilty' in a firm voice, but the judge directed a plea of not guilty to be entered. As he was shown to his seat in the dock, he buried his face in his hands and wept bitterly.

After outlining the circumstances of the case, Mr Lewis called as his first witness the victim's son, Thomas Welsh, who was also in tears as he spoke of coming to the house on Saturday and finding MacDonald attacking his mother. He said they were quarrelling about who owned the furniture, with MacDonald threatening to break everything in the house until she got up to wash, and he went to lie down on the sofa.

Next on the stand was Mr White, who had known MacDonald some thirteen years. The day before the murder, MacDonald gave him 3s, asking him to 'mind' it for him. He next saw him on the morning of Monday 29 June, at eight o'clock, when the prisoner came in for a drink. White told him it was too early but MacDonald insisted on having a pint of brandy, so White poured him out half that amount. He admitted he felt uneasy at the time, and some sixth sense suggested he ought to break in to the house later, when he found the bodies.

Sergeant Olwell testified going to the house shortly after the alarm was raised. Superintendent Brutton spoke of having charged MacDonald in the hospital with murder, while Constable Reep, also of Stonehouse Police, mentioned the letters found by the bodies. Thomas Pearse, the surgeon, gave medical evidence about the state in which he found the bodies of the couple.

Concluding the case for the prosecution, Mr Lewis suggested that there was no foundation for any suggestion of insanity on the part of the prisoner. The savage blows he had inflicted on his victim, following so closely on an assault the previous night, showed that the intention to commit murder was there. Any possible doubt there may have been about his plans must surely have been dispelled by the content of the letters he had left.

For the defence, Mr Collins contended that the demeanour and behaviour of the prisoner, when taken with the surgeons' evidence, raised a reasonable presumption that when he committed the murder he was not responsible for his actions. He believed that there should be an acquittal on the grounds of insanity.

In summing up, the judge reminded the jury of their responsibility in what was their 'most painful duty to discharge'. The question was whether the prisoner had intentionally struck Mrs Walsh with a deadly weapon, with intent to do her grievous bodily harm although not intended to kill her, or when he struck her did he intend to kill her? Such a crime might be reduced to manslaughter, and it was for the jury to assess the extent to which he had been provoked to strike the fatal blow. He believed there was no evidence which could reduce the crime to manslaughter. Their verdict must therefore be that he was guilty of murder, or else that he should be acquitted on the grounds of insanity.

The jury took only a few minutes to find MacDonald guilty. His attack on Bridget Walsh on the night prior to her death, and his farewell letters, both indicated a deliberate intention to kill, and they could not take issue with the prosecution's belief that he was perfectly sane at the time.

When the verdict was announced, the prisoner shook his head. He was lifted to his feet by warders as the sentence was passed, kept his head in his handkerchief, and cried bitterly. After donning the black cap, the judge told him that he had committed 'a wicked and cruel murder'. Although the prisoner had determined to try and take his own life, it was 'no excuse and no palliation whatever for your wicked and cruel deed.' Mrs Walsh had been a 'bad and wicked woman'; although the same could be said of him, he had no right to sit in judgement on her.

During the next few weeks a Roman Catholic priest visited MacDonald regularly. He acknowledged that it was a just sentence, and did not expect or want to be reprieved. In his last few days neither family nor friends came to see him. His parents were both still alive, and he declared that he would die a hundred deaths rather than that they should know what was to become of him. He made another will, in which he stated that the £11 which he still owned should be used to defray the expenses of Bridget Walsh's funeral, and the balance divided between her children, to be distributed at the discretion of her husband.

On the morning of 10 August he got up at about half-past five, washed and dressed, and made his bed. One hour later he received the priest, who stayed with him for about ninety minutes later, when he was pinioned and conducted to the scaffold. Holding a crucifix in his hand, MacDonald walked with a firm step to the scaffold where executioner William Calcraft was adjusting the rope which would, within a few minutes, launch him into eternity.

20

'TROUBLE ENOUGH I HAVE WITH HIM'

Exeter, 1879

In the spring of 1878, 29-year-old Mary Hoskins of Tuckingmill, near Camborne, found that she was expecting a child. Being unmarried, she was desperate to keep the news secret from as many of her family and friends as possible. Only her brother and sister were let into the secret, and she told everyone else that her health required her to have a change of air. In May she left Cornwall and moved to Exeter, taking lodgings in the suburb of Ide, under the name of Mrs Hede.

Four months later, she engaged a midwife, Mrs Down, to be ready when the time came. On 6 October, after a painful confinement during which she was at one stage close to death, she gave birth to a baby boy. He was registered as Reginald Hede, the son of Reginald and Mary Hede. When he was a few days old a doctor examined him and found the genitals were slightly deformed, although in all other aspects he seemed in good health. Mary was very fond of her baby son, and wanted to keep him, but her brother and sister put her under pressure to give him up.

One month later, on 9 November, her brother and sister, Mrs Tonking, came to visit her and suggested that she would do well to give the child up to a 'nurse', thus enabling her to return to Cornwall and make a clean start with her life. Mrs Tonking went to see Annie Tooke, who lived nearby at Bartholomew Street, and had placed advertisements offering to look after children, and arranged for her to take the child. She originally asked for 6s per week, but after some hard bargaining she agreed to accept 5s. Mrs Tonking gave her a down payment of £12, and a quantity of clothing, including a shawl and what was considered quite an expensive robe. Mrs Tooke was asked to keep the child for a year, but gave no clues as to the identity or whereabouts of the child's mother. A further payment was promised at the end of twelve months. The deformity was pointed out, and when Mrs Tooke asked whether it affected the child in any way, the latter assured her that it did not.

On 27 January, Mrs Tooke moved to the St Thomas area, and two months later she found lodgings in a house in South Street, near Exeter city centre. Four days later Mr Linscott, a pawnbroker in the city, took a child's robe, and on 24 April he received a shawl, both from a little girl who gave her name as Stokes. It was later found that the girl's real name was Bessie Tooke, Annie's daughter.

Apart from the minor deformity, little Reginald was a healthy baby, with an apparently insatiable appetite. On 25 April Mrs Tooke was writing to her daughter in Plymouth, complaining that the child was a great burden to her, and that she was clearly tiring of her responsibility, for which she considered she was being inadequately recompensed:

> I have dear baby – what am I to do with him, and trouble enough I have with him I can assure you. Dear little miserable child, you would never believe what food he eats. They say he overfeeds himself, and I believe it to be so. He has a cough like an old man.

Until then, she had occasionally been seen outside the house taking Reginald for some fresh air. One woman who saw them regularly was Mary Barrell, who lived at Alphington, but often came to visit friends nearby. She got to know Annie Tooke and always looked forward to seeing the baby, but last noticed him on 9 May. Five days later she called on Annie, saw her in her room, and noticed that cradle and child had both gone. When she remarked on this, Mrs Tooke said that Reginald had been taken from her by a 'strange woman'.

On 16 May Mr Preston, who lodged in the same house at South Street, met Mrs Tooke on the staircase, as she was coming out of her room. He was also a little uneasy about the sudden absence of the child, and remarked to her, 'I suppose you have arranged with the gentlemen about the child. I suppose it is a city case – it is going to the workhouse?'

'Oh dear no!' Annie answered. 'It is not in the workhouse at all. It is with a friend. I have to pay 4s a week for it.'

On the following day Edward Stookes, a miller, was clearing out equipment at the mill, when he made a horrifying discovery. Finding a bulky object submerged in the pond, he lifted it out and realised it was the headless trunk of a child. The limbs had been severed, with jagged cuts. A further search downstream next day revealed the missing head, arms, legs, and genitals. A surgeon, Dr Bell, examined the corpse and said that the baby was about seven or eight months old, and in good health apart from the deformity. Examination of the internal organs suggested that he had been last fed about an hour before death. There were portions of cinders adhering to the neck muscles. He took the portions to Mr Long, a photographer, who photographed the head, then had the pieces stitched together (which must have been an extremely harrowing task for whoever was called upon to do so), and took further photographs. They were shown to different people who had seen Reginald Hede while he was alive, and they all positively identified him.

When the news broke, Kate Rowe, who lived nearby, mentioned it to Mrs Tooke. 'What a dreadful thing about this baby,' Rowe said, 'they ought to be hung who done it.' She said that Mrs Preston had a newspaper carrying details of the story and the discovery of the body, and when Mrs Tooke denied having heard about it, she fetched it for her to read.

Enquiries into the murder were made and Mr Scanes, a butcher at Ide, who recalled seeing Reginald when he was handed over to Mrs Tooke, contacted the police.

A doctor who had known Tooke and the child and had seen them together also read about the murder. Not having seen the baby for over a week, he and the butcher called on her and asked her to produce young Reginald. When she told them that a stranger had called on her and taken him away about a fortnight earlier, their suspicions deepened. She denied that the murdered child was the one she had been looking after, but later admitted it was the same boy, while keeping to her story that somebody else had taken him away.

The police were aware of the mother's identity, and thought at first that Mary Hoskins had either taken her son away and killed him in order to save herself the money each week, or else been an accessory to the murder. On 22 May, Inspector Short called on Mrs Tooke and asked her to go with him to speak to Captain Bent, the Chief Constable of Exeter. When the latter questioned her, she said that she had given the baby to a woman aged about 50, 'with fully developed bosoms and a slender waist'. When he asked her if it was not rather odd for her to hand the baby over to a woman whom she did not know at all, she began to cry, saying how hard on her it was having all this trouble, as she was only a poor widow. Further questioning as to the child's parents elicited from her a description of members of her family who had left him with her the previous year.

Nobody knew enough as yet to charge her with killing the child, but suspicions were beginning to harden. Two days later, Inspector Short questioned her again. He showed her the photographs, and mentioned the child's deformity. She denied that they were of the child which she had been nursing, gave him an account of how she had handed him over, and gave the address. She said that they had taken away the child and every article of clothing that belonged to him. Short proceeded to search her house, and found a bill hook and razor, and at the same time saw a box with incisions and a dirty stain on it.

On 26 May, Mrs Tooke called on Captain Bent, and admitted that the photographs he had shown her were of Reginald Hede. On 4 June, Inspector Short went to Camborne to interview Mary Hoskins and Mrs Tonking, and next day he sent a telegram to Captain Bent, asking him to bring Mrs Tooke to Camborne. When they arrived there Mrs Tonking immediately Mrs Tooke. The identification formalities having been completed, they returned to Exeter.

Mrs Tooke gave Captain Bent a statement, describing how the child had been taken from her, and accused Miss Hoskins of murdering the infant. The latter appeared in court at Exeter Guildhall on 7 June, charged with being an accessory to her child's death, and Mrs Tooke appeared as a witness. When Mrs Tooke was asked in court how she came to part with the child, she said, 'They sent for it. Someone fetched it.' When asked who 'they' were, she did not know. All she could say was that it was 'a very respectable female.' When asked whether the baby had been given to her with a name, she answered in the negative, saying that she called him Percival. She also admitted to having no idea of the mother's name. Miss Hoskins was able to convince everybody of her innocence.

If the police had had any doubts that Mrs Tooke was not telling the truth, their suspicions were hardening. On 12 June, Inspector Short arrested her and charged her with murder. When asked if she had killed he child, she muttered, 'That you will have to trace out.' She was taken into custody, and her rooms were searched. Two shirts, a feeding bottle, and eighteen pawn tickets were found.

While in custody, sheasked to speak to Captain Bent. On 13 June she made a statement which she duly signed. She confessed to having murdered the child, admitted that her story about it being taken from her by a stranger was untrue, and gave details of how she cut the body up, and put the remains in a box. When she cut off the head, it fell over into the ashes in the coal hole, hence the cinders on it when it was found. Next day she had second thoughts, and wrote a letter in which she acknowledged having made her statement, but denied that it was the truth.

The two-day trial opened on 21 July at Exeter Assizes before Mr Justice Lopes, with Mr Bullen for the prosecution and Mr Matthews for the defence. As Mrs Tooke was brought into court by a warder and a schoolmistress from the gaol, she was in a half-fainting condition. She had fainted in the cells and swooned again before being arraigned. While she was in the dock, she had to be supported on either side when she was called upon to answer the Clerk of Arraigns, but still managed to give an audible plea of 'not guilty'. During the court proceedings, her hysterics regularly interrupted the evidence being given by witnesses.

Mr Bullen opened the case on behalf of the prosecution. He stated that Mrs Tooke had a clear motive in killing the child as she lived in utter poverty. She had received £12 for the child, yet did not expect any more money for another year. She was receiving parish relief, and had even pawned articles belonging to the child. Since the discovery of the body, she had made several contradictory statements, in addition to mutilating the remains of the infant left in her care and attempting to dispose of them. Edward Stookes, Mark Wingfield, William Benellick, Henry Searle and George Howard, the labourers who had found the portions of the body at different times, all took the witness stand to confirm having done so. Other witnesses called included Mr Bell, Mr Long, Mary Barrell, Mary Jane Down of Ide, and Elizabeth Tonking, who must have bitterly rued the day she had persuaded Mary Hosking to give up the infant.

Among the witnesses for the prosecution were Mr Bell, who had examined the bay twice in the few days after it was found. He said that in his opinion the child had not drowned, but was stunned by a blow on the back of the head, and then its throat was cut. It had been dead for several days before being placed in the river.

No evidence was offered by the defence, only cross-examination by Mr Matthews. After all the evidence was given, on the second day, Mr Bullen said in his summing up that he was sorry to find that there had been no effort on the part of the defence to mollify the evidence, or to tone it down in any degree, but he knew that such a task was impossible to undertake. He emphasised that the prisoner had made a statement admitting to the murder, and all her statements had been confirmed afterwards by the facts. On these facts, he concluded it would be for the jury to say whether or not they had established the guilt of the prisoner to their satisfaction.

Although the evidence against Annie Tooke was overwhelming, Mr Matthews summed up for the defence with a masterly speech in which he told the jury that Mrs Tooke would have found it all too easy to take the child to the workhouse, telling the authorities that it was an illegitimate child for which the parents had refused to provide. Why, as a mother herself, would she instead go to the lengths of murdering and mutilating a helpless baby when she could perfectly well have relieved herself thus of the responsibility and anxiety? Moreover, the evidence of the surgeon showed that a better nourished and more healthy child there could not be. When he sat down after speaking for seventy minutes, there was a gentle ripple of applause from the public galleries.

In summing up, the judge reviewed the evidence for the prosecution and the defence. He then reminded the jury that if they had any reasonable doubt as to the prisoner's guilt, they should give her the benefit of it, but if they believed that the evidence left no such doubt, they were bound to say she was guilty.

The jury retired for an hour, and came back with a verdict of guilty. When asked if she had anything to say, Mrs Tooke alleged that Captain Bent had sworn false evidence against her, and then thanked her counsel for everything he had done for her.

While she was held in the cells awaiting execution, she made a full confession in which she admitted that she had killed Reginald by smothering him with a pillow, and a few days later she dismembered the body with a hatchet and a knife in the coalbunker, before disposing of the remains in the mill. She was visited by her four children shortly before being hanged by William Marwood on 11 August.

21

'SAY NO MORE ABOUT IT'

Plymouth, 1879

Harriet Marker, who was born in or around 1849, was the daughter of a Plymouth lithographer. At the age of eighteen she married a Mr Lawrence, who rose to become a naval petty officer. He went to sea for several years, leaving her no financial provision and no choice but to support herself by her own industry. Many a woman in the same position would probably have turned to prostitution, but she was a skilled seamstress and soon found work as a dressmaker at Manchester and Liverpool. She moved several times, living briefly at Wigan, Rugby, London, and latterly at Chester. During this time she had at least two or three liaisons, one with another naval officer. There were two children, a son born before her marriage who took her maiden name and lived with his grandparents in Plymouth, and a daughter with her husband, who was being brought up by his mother.

In 1878 Harriet moved in with Alfred Gregory, a former soldier in the 22nd Regiment, who had just left the army and settled in a house at The Mews, Queen's Hotel, Chester. Aged between 35 and 40, he had a succession of rather brief jobs, including that of surgeon's assistant and as a cab driver. For a while they lived as husband and wife, and she took the name Mrs Gregory. During this time she worked as a barmaid at the Bear's Paw public house, and also as a dressmaker to various establishments. Both were heavy drinkers, and frequently quarrelled, much to the irritation of their neighbours.

At around this time Mr Lawrence was appointed a petty officer on board HMS *Bacchante*, an ironclad built at Portsmouth, which was to be remembered as the vessel on which the two sons of the Prince of Wales, later King Edward VII, served as midshipmen. Early in 1879, Lawrence returned from sea and visited his parents-in-law at their home in Anstis Street, Plymouth. This coincided with Harriet's decision that she had had enough of Alfred Gregory, who was not only becoming a hardened drinker but turning increasingly violent towards her. She left him, telling him that she was going to Australia. Whether she really had any intention of doing so, or whether she wanted to dissuade him from following her, was open to doubt. The most probable explanation was that she had decided to go back to Plymouth and stay with her parents for a while.

When she arrived there in June 1879, she was reunited with her husband. They agreed to put the past behind them, and try to make a new start together. Most importantly, he gave her his word that he would give her proper financial support in future. As he had been promoted in the navy, he would now be in a better position to do so. With her skills, Harriet quickly found herself employment at the local firm of Stidston, Moulder & Stidston as a dressmaker.

Meanwhile, back in Chester, Alfred Gregory, having been dismissed from his job as a cab driver, found new employment as a carriage cleaner at the Queen's Hotel. He asked around friends and acquaintances if they had any knowledge of Harriet. She had probably talked too freely to others of her real plans, and at length he found out that she had not gone to Australia after all, but was back in Plymouth. Determined to join her, he told his employer that he had urgent business and needed to go there at once. When he was warned that to do so could mean the end of his new job, he went regardless, travelling on the 4.25 p.m. train from Chester station on 5 July 1879.

On reaching Plymouth next morning, he went to her house, and she agreed to spend the rest of the day with him. Maybe she was having second thoughts and would be open to persuasion, as it might be assumed that if she was serious about shutting Gregory out of her life, she would have told him there and then that she did not want anything more to do with him. What happened that day is not recorded, but he probably did all he could to persuade her to go back to him. At any rate, she

Stonehouse Town Hall and police station, c. 1902. (© Simon Dell)

went back to her parents' home that evening, but not before he had wrung a promise out of her to meet him one final time the following day.

Early that next morning, 7 July, Harriet left the house, telling her parents she was going to work. She had, however, made arrangements with Gregory the previous day to meet him once again. At about half-past nine she joined him at the New Market Inn in Cornwall Street, at Stonehouse, where they went into a private room and ordered refreshments, a glass of ale and a ginger beer.

About twenty minutes later James Black, the assistant manager, heard a noise which sounded like a heavy weight falling. He thought it was from the street, and went outside to make sure, but everything looked quiet. As he came indoors he passed the room where the visitors had gone, and heard the faint sound of a woman screaming. Entering the room, he saw Harriet Lawrence lying against the table with her throat cut, and Alfred Gregory cutting his own throat with a razor. He ran to the front door and called for a policeman. A street porter, Charles Jordan, came at once to help. On entering the room he found Mrs Lawrence now on the floor, and Mr Gregory leaning on the table holding the razor. Mr Jordan tried to remove it from him, but Gregory muttered something inarticulate and they struggled before he broke loose, and inflicted a further gash on his throat.

Mr Black called a surgeon, Dr Meeres, who examined the bodies and confirmed that both had died from shock and loss of blood.

For the rest of that day, as soon as news spread, the New Market Inn was an object of curiosity to local sightseers. A crowd gathered around and stayed there for several hours, and the management had to draw down the shutters of the local rooms to keep inquisitive gazing at bay. The police locked the room which had been the scene of such tragedy.

That evening an inquest was held at the Guildhall by the coroner, Mr Brian. Among those who came forward to give evidence were Mr Black from the inn, Mr Jordan, the porter who had come in to assist, and Harriet Lawrence's father, James Marker. Letters had been found on the bodies of both. One of them, in Harriet's handwriting and discovered in Gregory's pocket, stated that she had become reconciled to her husband. She insisted that while she had liked Gregory, she had never loved him, and she implored him to forget her. A letter from him, written in what was described as a 'rambling' way, included the words, 'Say no more about it.' While this might have given the impression that he was prepared to accept her decision, his subsequent behaviour suggested the very opposite. He had meant to see her again and beg her to reconsider her decision,

and when she refused, he decided that if he could not have her back, then nobody else should.

One of the jurors, Mr Foot, said that he saw the couple entering the inn, and both appeared quite rational. There was nothing to show that Gregory was insane, but he would scarcely like to say that the man had been of sound mind. After some discussion, the foreman asked the jury if they thought he had been of unsound mind. Every hand was raised. There was no escaping a verdict that Harriet Lawrence had been wilfully murdered by Mr Gregory, who then committed suicide.

22

'NOT A TITTLE OF EVIDENCE AGAINST US'

Blackawton, 1884

Laura Dimes was born in 1861 at Oldstone, a mansion at Blackawton, about six miles west of Dartmouth, the youngest child of William and Martha Dimes. The family were very rich, and Laura wanted for nothing. She was said to be 'talented and beautiful' (although such a description was regularly applied to young women of the time), an accomplished artist and horsewoman. Yet a sheltered, privileged life in which she was financially dependent on her parents became stifling after a while, especially once her elder sisters had married and left home. Walking with her dog around the grounds and woodlands near the estate added to her feelings of isolation, and she must have dreaded ending up an old maid. The only way out

Oldstone, home of the Dimes family. (© Totnes Image Bank & Rural Archive)

would be to meet a charming young bachelor, but her opportunities to do so were limited. However, as she was a member of the local hunt, there was the chance of doing so at meetings and balls, and it was probably at one such occasion early in 1884 that she came across Hugh Rutherford Shortland.

Aged about 24, this dashing young man full of self-confidence was the son of Dr Edward Shortland, a former secretary to Sir George Grey, governor of New Zealand. He lived in Modbury, and had a local office at the London Hotel, Ivybridge, then sometimes known as Mallet's Hotel after the then proprietor. His profession was given as that of barrister, but most people only had his word for it. His name was connected with various business ventures in Devon, including mining enterprises, and plans to build a new railway line through the South Hams area, which differed from the projected one supported by other people and businesses in the area. His railway scheme was actively opposed, and he held several public meetings in south Devon at which he tried to impress on sceptical audiences the benefits of his proposals. While addressing one such gathering at Kingsbridge, he said some of his friends had amalgamated to establish a company which intended to run short lines through the Modbury district, and this would provide considerable local employment. At the same time he planned to purchase large tracts of land in Australia for the production of meat and cereals, business which would require him to leave England before long.

London Court, formerly the London Hotel, Ivybridge. (© Kim Van der Kiste)

Laura fell head over heels in love with him. He realised that as the daughter of a wealthy family, she would make the ideal wife for somebody like himself, who might require access to ready money. When she returned home and told her parents about this suitor, they did not approve, thinking him quite wrong for their daughter. As a grand family wedding was therefore out of the question, she and Shortland obtained a special licence. On 8 April 1884, Laura left Oldstone on horseback. Still in her riding habit, she and Hugh were married at Kingsbridge Registry Office.

There was never to be a honeymoon. Shortland told his new bride that he had a vital business appointment in New Zealand and needed to leave immediately, although there is some doubt as to whether this was broken to her that same day or within the same week, particularly as nobody else was ever party to the discussion. There was no question, he said, of her accompanying him. He returned to Modbury to make preparations, while she went back to Oldstone to tell her parents that she was now Mrs Shortland. Their reaction can only be imagined.

There she stayed, a lonely wife patiently awaiting her husband's return from the other side of the world. Just over a fortnight later she received a letter from him, and from Brindisi, sent to his solicitor in Plymouth and forwarded to Blackawton, saying that he was at Brindisi on his way to Australia, and that he would contact her again from Sydney, where his father was practising as a solicitor. This probably arrived on 28 April, the day that she went out on her usual morning ride around the estate. She returned to the house about midday, changed from her riding habit into a dress with straw hat, and took her collie Juno for a walk in the woods. When the dog later returned with no sign of its owner, it was assumed that she had gone to meet her husband. Mrs Dimes had been under the impression that her son-in-law had told his wife that his journey had been delayed, and she had gone to meet him.

Next day, Mrs Dimes went to the woods to look for Laura, but without success. A little later Elizabeth Luckraft, wife of the estate steward, took her dog to the woods for a swim in the pond. While there, she noticed a woman's hat just under the water, about 3 feet away from the bank. Looking closer, to her horror she saw a face beneath it, and ran to get help. A farm labourer returned with her, and hauled the body out. At once they recognised it as Laura Shortland.

The police were called and an inquest was held. Sergeant Mills of Blackawton confirmed that the deceased was fully dressed, and there was nothing to suggest any sign of a struggle or sexual assault, nor any sign that she had tried to get out of the water. The depth of the pond at the point where she was found was just over 6 feet 3 inches. Her dress had floated up to her knees, and the only possible indication of violence was a small, barely discernible bruise on her temple, so slight that it could not have resulted in any injury. Shortland's letter was produced and read out to those present. Largely in view of Mills's assertion that he had no reason to suspect foul play, the jury returned an open verdict of 'found drowned'. Nevertheless, they and the family were not satisfied that this was a satisfactory explanation.

An artist's impression of the discovery of Laura Shortland's body. (Illustrated Police News)

For the first few days, investigations revealed nothing. On 2 May William Ryder, who earned his living as an agent for Prudential Assurance in Plymouth and was an old friend of Shortland's, living in a small cottage nearby at Modbury with his father, near a tannery where he worked, and where Shortland used to stay from time to time, called at Mallet's Hotel to ask if any correspondence had arrived there for Shortland. There were no letters, they said; how could any be expected under the circumstances, and why did Ryder require them anyway? It appears that when Shortland had returned from New Zealand with his father on a previous occasion, the two young men renewed a boyhood acquaintance, with Shortland describing Ryder as his 'secretary'.

If Shortland had not sent Ryder to the hotel for the letters, it was likely that no further action would have been taken. Instead, the suspicion of first the management and then the police ensured that what had initially been viewed as an accidental death was now seen as something very different. The hotel manager reported his concerns to the police at Modbury. On 3 May, Constable Dunsford interviewed Ryder, who told them that he understood Shortland to have planned to leave Britain for Brindisi en route for New Zealand, and that he later received a letter from Shortland in Brindisi, containing a letter for Mrs Shortland. The envelope carried Brindisi,

London and Plymouth postmarks. All this seemed consistent with the evidence given at the inquest.

On the morning of 7 May, Ryder's father went to the Modbury police and informed them that Shortland was at his cottage, where he had been staying for a while. Constable Dunsford accompanied him back to the cottage and formally arrested Shortland on a charge of murdering his wife. A message was sent to Ryder at his office in Plymouth asking him to return, and when he did he too was arrested, charged with being an accomplice in Laura's death.

Subsequent police enquiries revealed that Shortland had never left Modbury, and that he had presumably been there within a day or two of saying goodbye to his new bride, before pretending to leave for his supposed journey to New Zealand. As far as they could establish, he had gone under cover of darkness to Ryder's cottage on 10 April at about ten o'clock in the evening, two days after the wedding, and Ryder's daughter was sent away from her home to make room for him. He claimed that he had stayed there until his arrest on 7 May. If this was true, he could not have murdered his wife on 28 April. He was, however, seen by a witness walking through the fields nearby on the morning of the day that his wife's body was found.

Both prisoners were aware of Laura Shortland's death. Doubtless in an effort to help create an alibi for his friend, Ryder told the police that when Shortland heard that his wife had died, he was so grief-stricken that Ryder himself took his razor and knife away so that he would not be tempted to commit suicide.

An examination of the banks of the pond in which Mrs Shortland's body was found failed to show any signs of a struggle. Then Mr Bond, brother of a farmer on one of the neighbouring estates, prompted by curiosity, examined the borders of the pond, and discovered some distinctly marked footprints about 2 feet from the water's edge. Similar footprints were observed near the oak tree on the right bank, at a point several yards from where the body was discovered, indicating that a man had apparently been in the pond. All this was passed to the police when they arrived at Oldstone and Superintendent Dore and his assistants went to the pond. Indentations in the mud and gravel bed were clearly made by a man, and it was thought that the pond might have to be drained before the enquiry was completed.

Nevertheless, on 15 May Shortland was charged at Kingsbridge Court with the murder of his wife, and Ryder with aiding and abetting him in the deed. Inspector Thomas Roots, of Scotland Yard, was the first witness to speak. He said he had obtained an order from the Home Secretary, Sir William Harcourt, for the exhumation of the victim's body, and had been present at the Dartmouth cemetery where two local doctors undertook a post-mortem examination. Parts of the body had been despatched to the government analyst at the London and Westminster Hospital, and a solicitor at the Treasury had written to him to request that they case should be remanded

Church Street, Modbury.

until a decision could be made. He was thus obliged to ask for a remand for eight days. A consultation was then held between the Bench and the acting magistrates' clerk. During this time the prisoner tried to make a statement to the court, but was prevented by his solicitor from doing so.

Inspector Roots had thoroughly covered the area between Blackawton, Ivybridge, Modbury, Kingsbridge and Dartmouth, and had had interviews with and taken depositions from everybody who was supposed to have seen Shortland since 10 April. He also spoke to Mr Mallet at the London Hotel. None of this added anything to his knowledge of the case, except that Shortland had never remained at the hotel for more than a day or two at a time, but had had permission to have letters addressed to him at the hotel, where they would be kept until he was able to call for them in person.

Roots had been advised of several rumours, in the course of his investigations and interviews, but had uncovered no firm evidence which would stand up in a court of law. The only proof that Shortland was ever seen outside the Ryders' residence from the time of his arrival on 10 April was that given by somebody living near the cottage. Inspector Roots intended to return to London at once, taking with him the papers found in Shortland's possession when he was arrested, as well as carefully prepared statements of depositions made by Robinson, the letter carrier, and Mrs Rogers, and various others. It was apparent that nothing else could be done in the case until the result of Dr Dupre's analysis was known. Should it fail to reveal any analysis of foul play, the police would have difficulty in presenting to the Kingsbridge Bench any case for justifying the further retention of Shortland in custody. If the analyst discovered anything of a positive character, the investigation would have to be resumed. The poisoning theory had not impressed the police authorities, and it might be difficult to establish firm evidence of any other misdemeanours.

Nonetheless, when the police searched Shortland's lodgings, among his papers they had found certain documents which could throw light on the case, particularly suggestions for counsel such as a lawyer would prepare prior to drafting a brief for use in a court of law. They contained protestations of affection for the deceased lady, and assertions of the writer's innocence of any responsibility for her death, as well as suggestions for proving an alibi in the event of any charge against him. They did not indicate any defence against any particular theory of death, but in a rather rambling fashion led the reader to believe that he wished to be considered innocent of any complicity in the murder.

Shortland's friends were convinced that events would prove that the cause of death was an accident. While admitting that his curious behaviour laid him open to suspicion, they thought it could be easily explained as being consistent with his well-known eccentricity of conduct in other matters, and they anticipated his being released from custody.

They insisted that it was not in his interests for him to murder his wife. There had been no marriage settlement, and he could therefore not profit by her decease. Nobody thought fit to suggest that Laura might have discovered or accused him in being involved with dubious business and threatened to go to the police. If this had happened, he would probably have been quite prepared to kill her and make the death look like an accident.

There was speculation around this time that there was no belief that analysis would disclose any evidence of poisoning, although some local doctors could only reconcile the appearance of the body when seen in the water with the administration of strychnine or some similar poison. Shortland was apparently unacquainted with the death of his wife until the Ryders brought him a newspaper article containing a report of the inquest on her body, when he told them he knew all about it. The police were unable to trace him to any point about the time that Mrs Shortland died, but they had ascertained that he was seen outside Ryder's house within a few days of it, and they had little hope of throwing any light on the case. Shortland's conduct in court was that of a very determined man, showing no sign of sorrow for his wife's death.

Shortland appeared on remand a second time at Kingsbridge on 23 May. Inspector Roots said that Dr Dupre's analysis was not yet completed, and he needed to ask for a further remand. If the court was adjourned for another eight days, the analysis might be completed by then. For the defence, Mr E.G. Bennett, a Plymouth solicitor, said there was no evidence against the prisoner, and he asked to be heard in opposition to the demand. The Bench ruled that this was not the time when any remarks could be made, and they accordingly declined to hear him. Despite Bennett's insistence that he had the right to be heard, the Chairman maintained that the decision of the Bench had been given, and ordered the removal of the prisoner. Shortland remained in the dock, trying in vain to address the Bench, but the Chairman repeated his

*The Laura Shortland case. (*Illustrated Police News*)*

instructions to the constable. 'This is persecution,' Shortland shouted as he was removed, 'there is not a tittle of evidence against us.'

On 31 May he was back before the Bench at Kingsbridge. Mr W. Golding again represented the counsel for the prosecution, with Mr Bennett for the defence. Mr Golding said that exhaustive enquiries had been made by Inspector Roots. He conceded that while these tended to remove suspicion from the accused, he only had himself and his 'eccentric behaviour' to blame for the position in which he had been placed, for the police being obliged to investigate the matter, and for the course which the magistrates had taken in remanding him, which became necessary in consequence of his suspicious actions. No post-mortem examination was made before the inquest, and therefore the belly had been exhumed, and the contents of the stomach submitted to Dr Dupre for analysis. There was no trace of poison or any other abnormality, it added nothing to the information already in the possession of the police, and therefore he did not propose to proceed any further.

Inspector Roots and the surgeon who had examined the body were both present, if the Bench should want to question either of them. Roots was sure that the legal advice of the accused must be glad the Treasury had made such an exhaustive enquiry, as it removed the suspicion which seemed to rest around Shortland.

Mr Bennett said that 'it was with considerable satisfaction that he had heard the statement of the Treasury solicitor, which did not necessitate the accused calling evidence to repel a charge the very name of which made every honest man shudder'. The prisoner had always repudiated this charge, and to this he was sure he would be able to give a positive denial. The Chairman, Mr Ilbert, said that the

Treasury had adopted a course with which the magistrates entirely acquiesced, and they should direct the discharge of the prisoner. At this there was a ripple of applause in court.

Mr Bennett then complained that the contents of certain letters taken from Mr Shortland by the police had been mysteriously divulged, and had appeared in a daily paper, thus causing considerable pain to the prisoner and his family. He believed the matter should be made the subject of an enquiry, but the Chairman said that it was not within the powers of the Bench to answer that. Meanwhile it was announced that Mr Ryder, who had been arrested for complicity in the alleged murder but had been acquitted for lack of evidence against him, had given Superintendent Dore of the County Constabulary notice of an action for false imprisonment.

Shortland was now a free man. Like Ryder, he attempted to pursue action against the authorities, and wrote to Kingsbridge Magistrates threatening them with criminal proceedings for wrongfully holding him in custody. Many people were convinced that his wife had been murdered – and he was one of them, maintaining that his wife had been killed and then thrown in the water.

Within a few weeks he had moved to Morley's Hotel, Trafalgar Square, from where he wrote a long letter to *The Times*. The newspaper did not publish it in full, but reported having received it, quoting briefly in the issue of 14 July that Shortland had commented on 'a general consensus of opinion on the part of all who have carefully and minutely weighed the facts that a murder of the vilest nature has been perpetrated'. In order to do justice to everyone concerned, he said that there had to be a fresh inquest 'of a more searching and satisfactory character than that which has been held', and he was intending to petition the Home Secretary on the matter. He wrote to the local press, in which he said he 'deemed it due to himself' as her widower to carry on the investigation in to Laura's death, as he had been confirmed in his opinion that she did not come to her death by accident or suicide. Medical experts whom he had consulted left him in no doubt that 'a most accomplished, depraved and audacious murder of the blackest and vilest villainy' had been committed. Although the analyst had found no evidence of poison in her body, he believed the doctors who suggested that her appearance in the water was consistent with her having been poisoned. It was apparent to him that 'an evanescent vegetable poison may have been administered, by way of perfume or otherwise, to the brain through the nostrils', and that her body may have lain in the grotto adjoining the pond, and then slipped in.

Having threatened the Coroner with a parliamentary enquiry for having prematurely closed the inquest, Shortland wrote to Edward Seymour, Duke of Somerset, Lord Lieutenant of Devon, with a long list of reasons why the investigation into his wife's death should be reopened. He appealed to him 'as the guardian of the peace of the county, to consider well these things and to provide against the repetition of such a foul crime as far as it is within your power...I plead not only as a husband but as a fellow countryman, crying out against murder of the foulest type, for its debased ability without detection and without punishment.'

All efforts and campaigns by Shortland and Ryder to claim any legal redress or reopening of the case proved fruitless. On 30 August, Shortland sailed for New Zealand. His activities there eventually landed him in a sexual and financial scandal, after he was found guilty of malicious libel against an unmarried woman, and sentenced to two years' imprisonment.

Mrs Dimes never got over the tragedy. Her health failed rapidly, and she died one year after her daughter. Mr Dimes followed her to the grave in 1891, leaving Oldstone to their son, William. Four years later, in February 1895, the house was destroyed when the kitchen chimney caught fire and spread rapidly throughout the rest of the property. The family evacuated in time and nobody was killed or injured, but only the outer walls of the house were left standing. It was a severe winter, with heavy snow making the lanes impassable, and no fire engines from Dartmouth or other nearby towns could reach the house.

In 1985 Laura Shortland's great-niece, Ursula Khan, wrote to local journalist and historian Judy Chard, who was carrying out research into the case. She told her she believed that Shortland had asked his wife to lend him some money as he was in financial trouble, and he arranged a rendezvous between himself or Ryder with her in the woods, where they would be away from the prying eyes of her disapproving family. She might therefore have confided the circumstances to her mother, who had become resigned to the marriage, or maybe even borrowed the money from her. When Laura failed to return, Mrs Dimes must have assumed that she had gone away with her husband. However, if husband and wife had quarrelled over money and she discovered his involvement in some shady if not criminal dealings, she may have drowned herself. Genuinely in love with her husband, she was desperately upset about his lying to her with regard to the journey to New Zealand and about his highly questionable financial affairs. Later generations of the family thought this most unlikely.

Had Shortland not met his wife in the woods, he could have been shocked and horrified when he heard of her death, and thought it best to hide until the inquest was over. If he had been there, they might have quarrelled; he struck her on the spur of the moment and then killed her. Yet bearing in mind the web of deceit he had already woven regarding his movements, he was probably capable of planning the murder in order to alleviate his money troubles, as well as to prevent her from going to the police, and laying low until he could go abroad.

To this day, the death of Laura Shortland remains a mystery. While accident could not completely be ruled out, such a scenario was improbable. It is hard to avoid the conclusion that she was almost certainly murdered, and that her killer staged 'the perfect murder' which enabled him to escape justice. Her widower was adamant that she had met a violent death, and it is hard to exonerate him from blame. If she was murdered, he was the most likely killer. Yet there was no solid evidence connecting him to the crime, and he was able to walk away a free man.

Another theory suggests that Shortland had never left the cottage at Modbury, except on the day of his wedding, and remained in hiding so he would not be seen.

He therefore sent Ryder as his go-between to ask Laura for a loan from family money in order to assist him with cash flow as a result of 'temporary' business difficulties. Ryder could not persuade her to hand the money over, so he beat her angrily on the head, leaving her bruised, then turned around to flee as she slipped in the mud on the edge of the pond and drowned. When another member of the Dimes family fell into the pond some months later, he or she was rescued with some difficulty as the water was full of weeds, from which even a conscious able-bodied person would have had difficulty in escaping without assistance.

Yet another theory is that Laura was killed with a poison which was almost unknown to British medical science at the time. Her father-in-law had published a journal in 1851 on his New Zealand travels, in which he referred to the stem of the poisonous *tutu* or *topakihi* fruit. The only known antidote was for the affected person to be kept below water until nearly drowned, and then rolled over on land until he or she was sick enough to eject the poisonous matter. Plants of the genus were found in southern Europe, and soldiers in the French army had died from eating the fruit while on a military expedition in Catalonia. Hugh Shortland would have been aware of the plant's poisonous properties, and could have acquired some on one of his visits abroad. For him to have poisoned his wife, carefully lowered her into the water where any traces of the poison in her body would soon have been eradicated, and then attempt to use his status as a son-in-law of the Dimes family to suggest an alibi, was not impossible.

More than a century later, the general view of true crime and local historians alike remains that he was the guilty man. Yet he managed to cover his traces and avoid being convicted for what might be called 'the perfect crime'.

23

'YOU HAVE MADE A GRAND MISTAKE'

Ottery St Mary, 1890

Elizabeth Mitchell, aged about 30, lived in a cottage at Lancercombe, Ottery St Mary, with her labourer husband and family. Their firstborn child died suddenly in early infancy, and was buried at St Mary's Church. Elizabeth never quite got over the bereavement. In March 1890 she gave birth to a daughter, and afterwards suffered from severe post-natal depression. At a time when such a condition was not readily recognised, during the next few weeks she was thought by her husband and friends to be 'weak and strange in manner'.

On 6 May, when she went to visit friends, she said she had put the baby in a tub, and that when she went home again afterwards, the five-week-old baby was found drowned in a pan of water in the cottage.

An inquest was held on 7 May at the house of Samuel Retter, who also lived at Lancercombe. Before proceedings were opened before Mr C.E. Cox, the deputy coroner, he said that the case was a very painful and serious one, and that he thought the mother should be afforded every opportunity of hearing the statements of the witnesses if Dr Francis Reynolds, assistant to Dr Grey, the usual family doctor, considered she was in a fit state to undergo the excitement. Dr Reynolds told the deputy that she had no objection to being present. As Mrs Mitchell took her seat, she looked very depressed and ill at ease, and at times she viewed the coroner and jury with a vacant look. During the course of the inquiry she made several barely intelligible remarks.

Mr Retter said that his son Charles, on coming home from Tipton on Monday, said his sister had told him that Mrs Mitchell had gone towards Sidmouth without her child. He went into the cottage, the front door of which was partly open, and finding the cradle empty, he went to the back kitchen, where he saw the baby with her clothes on in a zinc pan. The vessel was about ten inches deep, and the face of the child, lying on her left side, was completely submerged by water. He immediately took the child out of the pan and laid her on the floor. She had been dead for several hours.

John Ebdon, a road contractor from Harford, said that shortly before midday he had seen Elizabeth at Crosshill, apparently carrying an infant in a shawl. She approached him and asked, 'Have you seen a policeman here?' He told her that Sergeant Pope had just turned the corner in the direction of Sidmouth, and she said she did not want him particularly. Mrs Mitchell murmured other words which he took to imply that she required the police, and added, 'I must go; my dear baby is cold.' As a result, he was convinced that she was not 'exactly right' and seemed to be 'in great trouble.'

Dr Reynolds said he was called into the Mitchells' cottage about half-past five on Monday. He saw at once that the baby was dead, and her clothes were soaked, but there were no signs of violence on the body. From the post-mortem examination, it was clear that she had drowned. Earlier that day he had seen Mrs Mitchell, who told him in the presence of Sergeant Pope, representing the local police, that she had taken her baby down to the river, 'and when it cried I put my finger on its mouth. I took it out, and then I put it in the pan.' When asked if she had placed the child in the river, she said she had. The doctor had last seen Mrs Mitchell about two months previously, and had thought even then that she was 'wanting in intelligence' to some extent.

After the coroner summed up the evidence, the jurors held a short consultation and returned a verdict of wilful murder. One of them, Mr Perry, argued against the decision, saying that she was not in a sound state of mind. The coroner told Mr Perry that the question of sanity did not affect that jury, and said he was prepared to accept a verdict of wilful murder. Mrs Mitchell was then arrested after the inquest by Mr Pope, and taken to cells at the Ottery St Mary police station. Once there, she lashed out so wildly that it took several officers to restrain her.

Next day a special court was held at Ottery St Mary Town Hall. Elizabeth was escorted there by two policemen. Her sister, mother, cousin and various friends were all there in charge of her. At first she refused to sit down and tried to get out. The family held on to her, as she repeatedly shouted, 'You have made a grand mistake.' Once the proceedings had begun, she calmed down.

The first witness was Samuel Retter, who described his son's finding of the body and their reporting it to the police. Mrs Mitchell was asked if she wished to put any questions to him, and she appeared quite blank as she replied, 'Yes.' However she gave the impression of not really understanding what was happening, and she was about to make a rambling statement when the magistrates stopped her and called the next witness. Emily, the wife of farm labourer James Salter, who lived next door to the Mitchells, said she had gone into the house with Mr Retter and seen the dead infant. On the day in question, she said Mr Mitchell usually went to work early in the morning and came home to dinner at midday, but on this occasion he returned about three quarters of an hour later than usual. Mrs Mitchell herself had returned from Tipton about fifteen minutes earlier. Another witness, George Hellier, a wheelwright

of Tipton, said he had seen Mrs Mitchell later in the afternoon as she passed him on her way to Sidmouth, and she had nothing in her arms at the time.

Next was Emily, wife of Charles Barron, a cellarman, from Sidmouth, and Mrs Mitchell's cousin. She said that on Monday Mrs Mitchell had visited her in her house; she asked her what she was doing there, and Elizabeth said, 'You will think I am out of my mind.' Mrs Barron asked where the baby was, which she had brought with her on the previous visit. She replied, 'I have got it here,' putting her hand under a long cloak she was wearing. Mrs Barron unfastened it, only to find it was not there. Again she asked where the baby was. At first Mrs Mitchell refused to answer, then she said it was 'in the water.' Thoroughly alarmed, Mrs Barron went to Mrs Mitchell's house, to find the baby had just been taken out of the pan. During the night Mrs Mitchell was at the house of Mrs Barron's mother, and was very 'excited and troublesome'.

John Ebdon and Dr Reynolds both repeated the evidence which they had given at the inquest, and Sergeant Pope said he had arrested the prisoner and charged her with murder, then took her to the Ottery St Mary police station; on Thursday morning, in the presence of her sister, he again charged her, but she made no reply.

After all the evidence was given, the Chairman read the usual statement to the prisoner and asked her if she wished to say anything. She spoke a few incoherent sentences, but made no statement, and was committed for trial at the next assizes.

On 24 July, Mrs Mitchell appeared in the dock supported by two female warders. When she was charged she made no reply and her counsel, Mr St Aubyn, said he was instructed that the woman was insane and therefore unfit to plead. The jury were then sworn and the judge had to explain that the issue they had to decide was whether the prisoner was in sound mind and able to plead.

Dr Horton, of the Wonford House Asylum, said he had last examined the prisoner the previous week, found her in a very confused state, and did not seem to know anything. He questioned her about her child's death, but all she could tell him was that she had put it in the water. She did not know what was being said to her, but broke off into another subject. In answer to the judge, the witness said he did not consider she was in a fit state to plead. After a brief consultation, the jury decided that she was indeed unable to do so, and the judge ordered that she must be detained as a criminal lunatic in Exeter gaol at Her Majesty's pleasure.

24

'I'LL DO IT VERY QUIET'

Newton Abbot, 1896

Harry Grant joined the Royal Navy as a young man. What might have been a promising career was tragically curtailed at the age of twenty-six in October 1872, when he was travelling on a train. While stepping out of a carriage at Torquay, he fell between the platform and the carriage, and was so badly injured that in the course of treatment at the town infirmary an arm had to be amputated. There was no longer any place for him in the naval service, and he was invalided out. His family were convinced that he was never the same man since, both mentally and

physically. In April 1873, he tried to shoot himself and was brought before the magistrates charged with attempting suicide, but discharged. Later he found work as a painter.

In 1884 he married Sarah Raymond of Bovey Tracey and they settled in Lemon Road, Newton Abbot. For ten years they remained childless, until 8 September 1894, when a son was born. By this time, heavy drinking and increasing depression had taken their toll on Harry, and he suspected his wife was having an affair with

The River Lemon, Newton Abbot.
(© Derek Harper)

at least one other man behind his back. The baby, he believed, was not his. In the afternoon Mrs Catherine Massey, an upholsterer by profession an old friend of Mrs Grant, came to their house to help nurse the mother while she was resting after the birth. She was downstairs when she heard a loud scream and call asking her to come quickly. Going up to the bedroom, she found Grant standing over his wife in a threatening attitude, holding a brandy bottle above his head as if he was going to strike her.

'Don't let him kill me, take away the brandy,' she implored from the bed, lifting her left arm, and with the right one protecting the child. 'Take away the brandy, she'll drink all she can catch,' Grant snapped before going downstairs.

Next morning, while Mrs Massey was dressing the baby, Grant came up to the bedroom and demanded to look at it. He then sat down in a chair, saying to his wife, 'Sarah, you can have that bastard baptised what you like. Walter or Jack will do.' Sarah told him he was being very cruel, while the nurse told him firmly that Mrs Grant must not be worried.

'No, I won't worry her,' he said. 'I'll do everything I can for her and get her around, and I'll torture her like a cat tortures a mouse.'

The nurse stayed there for the next three days, during which Grant repeatedly called his wife a cow and other offensive names. Between January and April 1895, Mrs Massey looked after the little boy every day. On 30 March Mrs Massey, not having been home during the week, found Sarah at Mrs Massey's house, and they went together back to the Grants' house at Lemon Road. Mr Grant was in the kitchen, and Mrs Massey told him that she had come at his wife's request to tell him that she had been at her house all evening nursing the baby.

'It's not mine,' he said, 'it's a bastard.'

'You surely don't believe that,' Mrs Massey told him.

'If I did,' he told her, 'I wouldn't walk seven miles from Bovey after I left work to try and catch her.'

She asked him if he had ever seen Sarah with another man. He replied that he had not, and she remarked, 'Why don't you make them who say they have prove it? There is a police court.'

'Prove it?' he answered. 'I'll knock her brains out.'

'Perhaps you'll know better in the morning,' Mrs Massey added, 'then you'll talk different.'

'Perhaps you think I've been drinking,' he said, 'but I'm not, I'm ashamed to be seen out of doors.'

Sarah then broke in. 'I should think you was treating a wife as you treat me – coming in at shut-up time from the pub, rowing me, sitting in your chair, swearing yourself to sleep until three in the morning, and then coming upstairs threatening my life in bed.'

'Yes, and I'll catch you asleep yet and do for you,' Henry said threateningly.

'No you won't. If you knock me I'll call the police. There is generally one at the top of the road.'

'No you won't,' he retorted. 'I'll do it very quiet.'

Sarah said, 'Then you'll be hung.'

'No I won't; I'll do for myself as well.'

Fearful as to what might happen next, Mrs Massey took Sarah back to her own house, where Sarah stayed for an hour, when she felt it was safe to return home.

A week later, at about eight o'clock in the evening, Sarah went back to her house after visiting friends. She knew that her husband had been drinking, and that he would be in an uncertain temper, so she stood outside and watched him go in the opposite direction over the bridge. Even so, she knew that he could be back at any time, so she spent the next three hours with Mrs Massey. They then watched her husband return, and Mrs Massey agreed to come back with Sarah in case there was any trouble. When they arrived they found the door locked, and heard Harry indoors swearing loudly. As they could not get in, they waited outside until about midnight, when a policeman came along. He asked them what was going on, and after a brief discussion he suggested it might be safer, as well as causing less disturbance, if Mrs Grant returned to Mrs Massey's house for the night. They agreed this was the best solution.

Other residents nearby often heard angry words between Harry and Sarah. Not long after the boy was born, John Blatchford, a corn merchant who lived a few doors away from the Grants in Lemon Road, heard them quarrelling in the house, then saw Sarah running down the yard, followed by Harry. As soon as he saw Blatchford watching he stopped, turned back and went back into the house. Meanwhile, Sarah jumped over the wall, and next morning Mr Blatchford heard that she was so terrified that she had spent the night in the house next door.

From that time on, Harry's behaviour steadily deteriorated. In April 1895, when Sarah went to visit another neighbour, Harry came round and dragged her away without any explanation. When the neighbour told him he ought to be ashamed of himself, he said he would knock her brains out.

Husband and wife were now living an increasingly miserable existence, with Sarah doubtless wondering how much longer she had to put up with his heavy drinking, bad temper, verbal abuse, and threats of violence. Release from such a life was not long in coming, though certainly not in the way she would have wished.

On 18 July, Harry Grant made a will, in which he left all his possessions to his elder sister, Mrs Jane Zaple, of Torquay.

About three weeks later, on the evening of 8 August, he returned home at about half-past eleven, very drunk. A passer-by heard him quarrelling loudly with his wife, calling her offensive names. Shortly before eight o'clock the next morning, he came out of his house into the yard, and then returned, locking the door after him. About half an hour later he went to the railway station, and threw himself towards a moving train on the platform. If the subsequent testimony of neighbours was to be believed, this was one of several suicide attempts since that of April 1873. Once more, he was badly but not fatally injured, and was taken to the local cottage hospital for treatment.

Newton Abbot railway station. (© Derek Harper)

Later that day Sarah was found in the house, unconscious, with six wounds on her head, and a coal hammer on the floor beside her. She was also taken to hospital, where she lingered for another two days before dying.

On 12 August, Sergeant Coles went to see Harry in hospital and formally charged him with the murder of his wife, but Grant made no statement at that stage. Sarah Grant's funeral was held at St Mary's Church, Wolborough, on 14 August. An inquest into her death was opened and adjourned until the last week of August, in the hope that her widower would be well enough to attend, have an opportunity of hearing the evidence read to him, and be able to question the witnesses. However, Dr Stanley Stevens, who was in charge of him, was unable to tell the court when he would be released from hospital, and it was decided to proceed regardless.

Among the witnesses called were Dr Stevens, Mrs Massey, and several neighbours, including a local cab driver. The latter testified to having seen Harry Grant on Sunday morning, and to his having wished them all good morning or spoken otherwise briefly to them. None of them said they noticed anything unusual about his manner. Sergeant Coles said that Harry Grant had been asked in hospital whether he intended to have a solicitor, but he said that he had no means and that 'he didn't see the use of it'.

St Mary's Church, Wolborough, near Newton Abbot, where Sarah Grant was burined in 1895.
(© Derek Harper)

On 8 September, Grant, now out of hospital, was charged at Newton Abbot Police Court. He had his remaining shattered arm in a sling, and his head was still bandaged. (According to one report, his second arm had had to be amputated as well.)

Catherine Massey was the first to take the witness stand, and gave a history of the problems between husband and wife from the birth of their son onwards. She was followed by Maria Street, the wife of a fisherman living in Teignmouth, who had known the couple for about nine years. She said she had met Mr Grant in July in Newton Abbot and they went for a drink together. In the course of conversation, he said to her, 'Times are not not what they were then,' adding that his wife – 'that cow of mine' – was nothing but 'a common whore'. Mrs Street tried to persuade him that he was mistaken. He then told her that Sarah was in the habit of going to bed between eight and nine o'clock, and he had walked home while working at Bovey with the object of catching her, and had found that instead she came home about 11.30 p.m., frequently the worse for drink. She always excused herself on the grounds that she had been at a neighbour's house. One night, he followed her up Powderham Road, and when he caught up with her, she told him she was going to get her clean clothes, then turned and walked home with him.

Grant told Mrs Street that he thought she was going there for some other reason. 'If I do catch her I know what it'll be; I shall kill her.' Street told him firmly, 'Don't let that anything like that enter your mind. It is better for you both to part if it is like that.' Grant replied, 'Don't be frightened to hear any time that I have, or have done something very bad.' It was the first time that he had ever confided in her about any trouble between himself and his wife.

Another friend, Susan Hales, said she had known the couple for some years. Mrs Grant often visited her at her house at Lower St Paul's Road, Newton Abbot. She had been looking after the Grants' son for the last eighteen months.

William White, landlord of the Devon Arms, said that Mr Grant had often come to his inn, usually on a Saturday or Sunday. He had witnessed the will made on 18 July, which Grant had asked him to take care of, and also asking him to communicate with the address on the front if anything should happen to him.

John Blatchford testified to hearing the couple quarrelling regularly. About a month before Sarah was killed, he heard them arguing fiercely late one night, Grant telling his wife that 'I'll do for you before long,' to which Sarah replied, 'No you won't. All that I want you to do is to knock me, but you know better than to do that.' On 9 August, just after ten o'clock in the morning, Blatchford saw a crowd gathering outside Grant's front door. He fetched a ladder and placed it against the upstairs window, which was open about eighteen inches from the bottom. Constables Ashley and Creech went up the ladder and entered the room, with Blatchford and Henry Shepherd following to assist the police and doctors in the house, where the body of Mrs Grant was discovered lying under the bed.

Other neighbours gave similar evidence about arguments between the couple, before the inquest was adjourned to give Grant the opportunity of hearing the evidence read over and question the witnesses if he so wished. When it was resumed later in the week, only two witnesses were left to be called. Grant's solicitor, Mr F.J. Carter, was present, and said that acting under his advice, no questions from his client would be put.

The main witness was Grant's sister Jane, wife of Frederick Zaple, carpenter, of St Marychurch, Torquay. She spoke of Harry's naval discharge and first suicide attempt, and that in her opinion he had been deranged since losing his arm on that occasion. She had never witnessed any quarrels between him and his wife, adding that three weeks after her confinement Sarah Grant had said that he had acted very kindly towards her, and could not have been more attentive.

The surgeon, Dr Grimbly, who practised at Newton Abbot, said that Grant had been his patient for the last six years, and had always been of an irritable temperament, quickly roused to passion without good reason, and subject to moods of severe depression. Asked by Mr Carter if he considered from his mental condition that he could be responsible for the murder, the surgeon said that Grant might, in the heat of temper and without being able to stop and reflect, commit such an act for which he would be scarcely responsible. The irascibility might have been brought about by some brain disorder, which had been aggravated since his arm was amputated.

In summing up, the coroner said it was for the jury to consider the evidence given before them. Unless there was clear evidence to satisfy them that there was no malicious intention in his killing her, they could not reduce the crime to manslaughter. There was no witness to the crime, and a large amount of circumstantial evidence. None of the witnesses who met and spoke to Grant on the Sunday morning noticed anything abnormal about his behaviour, yet there was evidence to show that he had a motive in that he was dominated by the idea that his wife had been unfaithful to him. The jury retired for ten minutes before returning a verdict of wilful murder.

The case came to trial on 16 November at Exeter Assizes before Mr Justice Wills. Mr J. Alderson Foote and Mr E. Percival Clarke prosecuted, while Mr H.E. Duke defended. Grant pleaded not guilty to the charge.

After opening the evidence for the prosecution, Mr Foote called on witnesses, including Alfred Rowell and Henry Winsor, who both lived a few doors down from the Grants in Lemon Road. Between them, they said that Grant had always been quick-tempered, even sulky, but they never saw any evidence of his being jealous of his wife or suspecting her of infidelity. However, as soon as he began talking about anything, he lost his temper. Henry Wedlake, who lived next door to the Grants, said that for a month before Sarah Grant was killed, the couple had been quieter. He confirmed that Grant had been employed by Great Western Railway as a painter, and he had heard rumours that he had lost his job because people were afraid to have him, but he could not confirm these tales.

Dr P.H. Deas, medical superintendent of Wonford House Asylum, who had examined Grant at the request of the court, said that in his opinion Grant was not insane, but that his mental condition was unstable at the time of the murder. Grant spoke 'naturally and regularly', and gave no sign of incoherence or delusion, and his

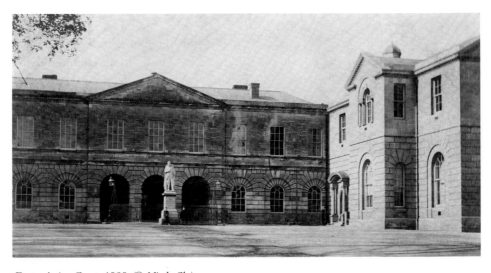

Exeter Assize Court, 1909. (© Nicola Sly)

memory seemed good. His manner was depressed and he broke down sometimes. The gaol surgeon said he thought the prisoner was perfectly sane. A slightly different opinion came from the superintendent of the Devon County Lunatic Asylum, who thought that Grant inherited from both sides of the family 'a strong tendency to melancholia, with active suicidal impulses from time to time', and that in all probability he was morally and legally irresponsible at the time of the murder. He was not fully responsible for his actions, as there were circumstances to which he had been subjected from accident or disease, or both, which had rendered him mentally unstable and diminished his powers of self-control, and in his opinion he was not fully responsible.

The prisoner's sister, Mrs Zaple, began weeping as soon as she entered the dock, and was given a seat. She said that insanity had existed within the family. Their mother had suffered from depression and epilepsy, especially in her later years, while a cousin of their grandparents had also been insane. She said that in conversation, her brother sometimes gave the impression of not taking any notice, but appeared dazed and lost. Four years earlier, he had jumped into the River Lemon at Newton Abbot, with portraits of their parents in his pocket.

In summing up, Mr Foote said that seldom had there been a case where the facts were less in dispute. Could the jury, he asked, come to any other conclusion than that when the prisoner was striking a blow, he knew he was striking one on a human being of flesh and blood? Mr Justice Wills said he thought the grounds on which the prisoner was said to be legally insane were slender enough.

The jury found Grant guilty, but with a recommendation to mercy. The judge sentenced him to death, promising that the recommendation of the jury should be sent to the Secretary of State. Three weeks later, on 4 December, the Home Secretary commuted the sentence to one of life imprisonment.

25

'A FEW SWEETS AND SOME OXO CUBES'

Whimple, 1938

By the New Year of 1938, Police Constable John Tremlett Potter, aged 46, was about to celebrate twenty-five years of being in the Devon Constabulary and then retire. He became a police cadet in 1913, joined the army two years later, and returned to his chosen career in 1919. A conscientious officer much respected by colleagues, citizens and even some of the villains, he had been stationed in several Devon parishes, and was now stationed at Whimple, a quiet village to the north of Exeter. He, his wife Agnes and their 18-year-old son William lived at the police cottage in the village. The local crime rate was very low, and the family were much liked and respected as part of the local community.

Being so well known, PC Potter had several friends and informants who kept him informed of any possible crimes, or anything untoward occurring in the area. Towards the end of 1937 he was advised of petty pilfering at the premises of the Whiteway's Cyder Factory at Whimple, where his son worked. While off duty he tried to collect some information about the thefts from the factory, but proved unsuccessful. From this he drew the conclusion that any crime was probably being committed by criminals outside the district, maybe coming in and going out via the railway line next to the factory.

On 17 January 1938, PC Potter was working a split shift, the second part being between 8 p.m. and midnight. As he was keen to keep an eye on the factory, he left home at around 7 p.m., telling his wife that he would walk to Knowle Cross and return home for supper about 9.30 p.m. He took a torch, but left his truncheon and handcuffs behind. When he failed to arrive home for supper, his wife and son were not unduly worried. They assumed that he must have been called to attend an incident, and were sure that he would be back shortly after midnight.

They went to bed at the usual time, but Mrs Potter was increasingly uneasy when her husband failed to arrive home, and soon after midnight she was sure that

The house in Whimple where Constable Potter and his family lived. Note the words 'Devon Constabulary' over the door. (© Simon Dell)

something must be wrong. John always notified her if he was going to be back late. She woke William, and contacted the local police station at Ottery St Mary. Sergeant Abrahams answered the call, and agreed to come to Whimple so he could undertake a thorough search of the area.

William Potter was sure that his father must be in the vicinity of the cider factory. He went there at once, and checked the outside areas thoroughly, but found no sign of him. The factory was locked at night, as was the main office door. Everything looked secure, and there was no sign of anybody or anything wrong.

He returned home and spoke to Sergeant Abrahams, who had brought a colleague, Constable Lamb. They ascertained PC Potter's usual route on his beat, and any particular concerns which he may have had at the time. William Potter told them about the thefts at the factory, and mentioned that he had already been there but seen nothing suspicious. Both officers and William went out for a drive around Whimple and the surrounding district, hoping they might see the constable on their way. They visited Talaton, a village two miles east, and questioned everyone them met, but nobody had seen the missing constable. Householders were awoken and questioned, but nobody had seen PC Potter since mid-morning the previous day. As time went on, everybody became more anxious. In case he had been knocked off his bicycle on a narrow country lane, the ditches and hedgerows were searched, but this revealed no trace of him either.

That afternoon, they carried out a thorough search of the railway yard and the exterior of the factory office areas. It then crossed their minds that Potter might have been having problems at home, and there was no way round it but to interview his wife. She could not identify any issues of this nature.

Whiteway's Cyder Factory, scene of the attack on Constable Potter, which resulted in his death sixteen days later. (© Simon Dell)

The offices where Constable Potter's murder was investigated. (© Simon Dell)

Constable Potter's helmet at the murder scene in Whiteway's office. (© Simon Dell)

When the next working day started at about seven o'clock in the morning, the managing director, Ronald Whiteway, arrived at the cider factory. As the keyholder, he needed to come and open the staff entrances, and he opened the main office door first. As he entered the building, he was surprised to see that the office door was open. He stepped in further and saw a policeman's helmet on the floor. As he switched on the light, he was astonished to see the office in a state, with the desk ransacked, papers all over the floor, and the whole place covered in blood. In the middle of the floor was Constable Potter, his uniform soaked in blood, and seriously wounded in the head. Moments later William Potter arrived for work and was, naturally, even more horrified. Whiteway tried to shield him from the worst of it, and sent him to find Sergeant Abrahams.

Potter was immediately transferred to the Royal Devon and Exeter Hospital, as the hunt for his attackers began. Meanwhile, Sergeant Abrahams went to report the incident to police headquarters, and Detective Inspectors West and Harvey were sent to Whimple, arriving later that day. Major Lyndon Henry Morris, Chief Constable of Devon, visited the scene, while Scenes of Crime personnel also visited the factory and carried out a thorough examination of the area. On an office window, they found a set of fingerprints which were lifted and retained as possible evidence.

The workforce were interviewed about their movements on the previous night. The trail led them to Leslie George Downing, aged 26, who lived at Burnthouse Lane, Exeter. He was interviewed on 19 January and the fingerprints on the office window were identified as his. When the detectives spoke to him, he explained that a fellow employee, 27-year-old Stanley George Martin, of North Street, Ottery St Mary, had also taken part in the incident. Both men, who had worked in the bottling department at the factory for about ten years, were married with young families.

In his first statement, Downing said that he swore he never saw Constable Potter on the night of 17 January, and that blood found on his coat came from four chickens which he had taken from Mr Whiteway's coop at the back of the orchard, and he had killed them by banging their heads against the trees. In a second statement he admitted that he and Stanley Martin had both decided to break into the factory to look for anything worth stealing, taking Martin's cycle lamp with them. He got into the office through the window, and opened a door to admit Martin. Constable Potter, he said, must have been waiting outside. They found nothing worthwhile in the office areas, so they stole a tin of meat extract cubes instead. As they were leaving the factory office area via the front door, they were confronted by Potter, who spoke to Martin and seemingly failed to see Downing, who was hiding behind a door. At once there was a violent confrontation between both men, which allowed Downing to escape. Having had no involvement whatsoever in the attack on Potter, he ran out to the railway station and caught the 9.28 p.m. train to Exeter. He insisted that he knew nothing about the latter's injuries until the following morning when he spoke to Martin, who had cuts and bruises on his face; 'I asked him whether he did it – meaning "bumping the constable". He told me he had done it in a struggle.'

If he was speaking the truth, then Leslie Downing had identified the assailant and the motive behind the attack. All that was left for the investigating detectives to do was to put these allegations to Stanley Martin in order to check his response and confirm or deny Downing's involvement in the matter.

When Martin was interviewed and made his own statement, he made no attempt to deny the allegations against him, but agreed with Downing's version of events. He explained that as they were leaving the factory via the main door, Potter had run in and grabbed hold of him, resulting in a fight:

I had to defend myself as best I could. Downing disappeared while we were struggling in this office. The constable tried to pull me out and switched on all the lights. He had a torch in his hand and kept on hitting me with it. He just said, 'I know who you are,' and I never said a word. I hit him with my fist. He grabbed my light away from me before I picked up the chair, and afterwards he tried to blow his whistle, but I pulled it away from him. We kept on and on until I was pretty well done in, and then he fell to the ground and couldn't get up again, but he kept moving on the floor.

PC Potter. (© Simon Dell)

Once Potter gave up the struggle Martin fled, locking the front door behind him and leaving his victim helpless on the floor, and when he was outside he threw the police whistle away. He later took police officers to the place where he had thrown it, and where it was subsequently found. At the same time he corroborated Downing's statement that the latter did not take any part in the assault.

Both men were arrested, cautioned and charged with causing grievous bodily harm with intent to murder Constable Potter. While neither of them positively denied the charges made against them, it was apparent that Downing was guilty of burglary yet innocent of the assault charge.

Meanwhile, John Potter was still in a critical state in hospital. His injuries included wounds behind the left ear and on the forehead, a fractured skull, and a deep cut beneath the right eye. He remained unconscious for a further sixteen days, and at first there was hope that he would recover, but on 30 January he had a relapse. Two days later his condition had become critical, and Agnes remained at his bedside until half-past seven on the morning of 2 February, before leaving her vigil, exhausted, to get some sleep. By then he was sinking fast, and died two hours later. The official causes of death were given as pulmonary embolism, a depressed fracture of the skull, laceration of the brain, haemorrhage and shock.

The charge was now one of murder, and both Martin and Downing were charged at Ottery St Mary on 4 February. The case for the prosecution was opened before the magistrates in the town court seven days later, the prisoners' statements were read, and evidence was called for the prosecution. At a further court appearance before the magistrates one week later, they were committed for trial at the Central Criminal Court, London, charged with murder, breaking and entering the premises, and stealing. Downing said that he was innocent, while Martin said nothing. Downing's solicitor, Mr S.E. Crosse, submitted that there was no *prima facie* case against his client on the murder charge. Most of the evidence against him was in respect of the alternative charge of breaking and entering, which he was not contesting in any way. The Bench ruled against Mr Crosse's submission and committed both men for trial on charges of murder and office-breaking.

Asked if he had anything to say to this, Downing replied that, 'Only on the charge of murder. I repeat I am innocent.' Martin then said, 'To intentional murder I am not guilty.'

The trial began on 21 March before Mr Justice Hawke, with Mr Reginald Powell Croom-Johnson, KC and Conservative MP for Bridgwater, and Travers Christmas Humphreys appearing for the prosecution, Mr John Graham Trapnell and Henry Elam for Downing, Mr Joshua David Casswell, KC, and Mr T.N.C. Burrough for Martin. Both

Mr Reginald Powell Croom-Johnson, KC, prosecuting counsel at the trial of Martin and Downing.

men pleaded not guilty to murder. Croom-Johnson outlined the sequence of events, culminating in the death of Potter, and quoted from Downing's two statements. When he read the part in which Martin confessed to having 'bumped' the constable, his counsel declared that this was no evidence against Martin.

Martin's statement was then read. In conclusion, counsel for the prosecution said that if a man killed a police officer in the legal execution of his duty the law implied malice, and the offender therefore became guilty of murder. If two persons, both engaged on an unlawful occasion together, decided that they were going to resist arrest, then every act which was done in pursuance of the common purpose was done by both.

On the second day evidence was heard by Dr W. Robb, pathologist at the Royal Devon and Exeter Hospital, Detective Inspector Harvey from Torquay, and Detective Inspector West from Exeter. They all discussed the nature of Potter's injuries, and the fact that blood had been found on Downing's coat (which he had been given by his mother-in-law just before Christmas), but none on Martin's clothing. Next day it was the turn of the defence, with Downing and Martin both speaking on their own behalf. They spoke of what had happened when they broke into the factory. According to Martin:

> [Constable Potter] flashed his light on me. I turned to make quick leave of the premises but I cannoned into the partition and the policeman caught me by the coat sleeve. He switched on the main light. I struggled to get away and pulled him into the director's room. The next minute I felt a stunning blow on my forehead from the torchlight. Blood was running down my face. His helmet went, but I did not see it go. I felt a bit angry and started to go for him with my fists. In the passage he gave me another blow on the head with the torch. I fell back against a picture and heard what sounded like glass falling. He tried to pull me to the door, but I resisted and pulled him into the clerk's office. There it started into a free fight. He was using his fists and I hit him on the head with a bicycle lamp. That seemed to make matters worse.

In his defence, Casswell remarked that Martin weighed only 11st 6lb, while Potter was 15 stone. Martin then continued that before he hit the constable with the chair, which he used after the lamp, Potter was getting the better of the fight. If he had realised how seriously he had injured Potter, he would have immediately gone for assistance. He had known him a long time, and neither owed each other a grudge.

On the fourth day, evidence for the defence was completed. For Martin, Casswell submitted that it would be for the jury to decide whether more force was used by the constable than was necessary to arrest Martin, and that what began as an arrest actually became a fight. In that event, counsel told the jury they could reduce the charge to manslaughter. If a policeman was using excessive force, he was in the same position as an ordinary civilian. If he exceeded his duty and took part in a fight, that would be a matter for the jury's consideration, even if he decided to revenge himself because he had been personally injured. For Downing, Trapnell said that there was no evidence of Downing's going to do anything other than to commit robbery.

Replying for the prosecution, Mr Christmas Humphreys submitted that there was no evidence of manslaughter. There was not a single item in Martin's evidence which changed the application of the law as laid down for several hundred years, that if a man killed an officer of justice in the legal execution of his duty the law would imply malice. The counsel submitted that Martin was actually arrested and was trying to get away when he was struck. As the constable did not have a truncheon with him, he used a torch, which was the next best thing he had with him at the time. With regard to Downing, counsel said that the prosecution were prepared to stand or fall on whether he was taking an active part in the fight. That, said Mr Justice Hawke, would be a matter for the jury.

Addressing the jury, Trapnell said that they were being asked to convict Downing of murder merely because of the bloodstains on his coat. If they accepted the submission of the defence – that there was another possible origin of the blood – then they should not convict. If it had come during the struggle, how come there was no blood on Martin's clothing? He submitted that Downing could not be guilty because he was not there, and that the only verdict possible was that he was not guilty.

Casswell asked the jury if, 'when Martin set forth on that silly pilfering exercise,' he thought it would lead to him being put in the dock? Did they think Martin looked like a gunman going forth to kill? If the policeman had had his truncheon with him, it would have been over quickly. The proper verdict, he suggested, was the merciful one; that they should say it was not proved that the man, unprovoked, has killed a police officer in the course of his duty. The defence thought the policeman had gone beyond the course of his duty, and the result was a fight, and that Martin was guilty of manslaughter, but not of murder.

Before beginning his summing up, the judge said that there seemed to be a suggestion that Martin, being a rather inarticulate and not very well-educated Devonshire lad, had not been able to express himself clearly. Did they think he showed any signs of confusion or difficulty when he gave evidence?

On the fifth and last day, 25 March, after all the evidence had been heard, the judge said that that the substantial evidence that Downing was present at the attack was the matter of bloodstains on his coat. The jury could assume that he did not know the stains were there, or he would not have worn the coat to work the next day. There was nothing to indicate when he reached the railway station that he had been engaged in the deadly struggle of which the jury had heard. Martin had testified that Downing disappeared when the Constable arrived, and if that was true, whatever was found on Downing's coat was not the blood of the dead man. If the jury were satisfied that Downing was not present at the attack, they should acquit him.

In summing up, he remarked that 'the terribly pathetic thing about this case is that all this should have arisen out of a few sweets and some Oxo cubes.' The jury might think that Potter had used excessive force, and if so, the proper verdict was manslaughter. If Martin had killed him to resist arrest, it was murder.

It did not take the jury long to agree that Downing was not guilty of the charges of murder and manslaughter, and on these he was accordingly discharged. The only charges which could be brought against him were those of office-breaking and burglary, for which he received twelve months. No such verdict could be returned where Martin was concerned. In finding him guilty of murder, they added a very strong recommendation to mercy, on the grounds of his previous good character and the fact that he obviously did not intend to commit murder. They expressed sympathy with the family of Constable Potter, and urged that in future no policeman should go on duty without his truncheon for self-defence.

Nevertheless, Martin was found guilty, and sentenced to death. He appealed against the sentence, claiming he had no actual intent to kill and had no obvious weapons with him when the crime was committed. On 2 May, the Court of Criminal Appeal dismissed this, but eleven days later the Home Secretary, Samuel Hoare, commuted the sentence to one of life imprisonment. Had the execution gone ahead, it would have been on the same day as his daughter's second birthday.

The headstone of Constable John and Agnes Potter at St Mary's Church, Whimple. (© Simon Dell)

In Devon, many donations were made to a subscription fund started by police officers across country, and £740 was raised for PC Potter's widow and son. Whiteway's donated a small plot of land on which a house was built as a permanent residence. Agnes Potter survived her husband by fifty years, and died in December 1988, aged 95. She was laid to rest beside him at St Mary's Church, Whimple.

26

'YOU CAN HAVE HER BACK WHEN I'VE FINISHED WITH HER'

Exeter, 1941

It has been said that wartime was often accompanied by a general loosening of morals. Husbands were away for months at a time, sometimes destined never to return, and women were desperate for company, while adults of either sex were anxious to live for the moment as there might not be too many tomorrows. The Second World War, therefore, saw more than its fair share of broken marriages. Occasionally it developed into something even worse.

At about 11.30 p.m. on 19 August 1941, the constable on evening duty at Exeter police station received a telephone message concerning an incident at the Elephant Inn, North Street. Several officers went to the inn and arrived at midnight. They were shown into a bedroom where a body was lying on the floor. On a bed nearby was a revolver. The dead man was Montague Ridge, a NAAFI manager, and he had been shot several times.

Enquiries were made, and it emerged that Ridge had been having an affair with Blanche Emmert of Cedars Road, whose husband, Frederick, was a 46-year-old civil servant. When Emmert confronted Ridge and asked him to break off the affair, the latter seemed quite unashamed of his behaviour. 'You can have her back when I've finished with her,' he retorted. That evening Emmert had gone to the hotel to reason with him and again asked him to stay away from his wife. The two men talked for about twenty minutes, but Ridge proved obdurate and refused to leave her. Eventually Emmert, provoked beyond endurance, took out his revolver. Whether he had intended to kill the man who had stolen his wife, or fired in the heat of the moment, only he would know.

Constable Lindsey arrested him, and took him to the police station where he was charged, cautioned and made a statement. On 21 August he appeared at the magistrates' court to hear the charge. When asked by the clerk, he said he had no reason to advance why the case should not be adjourned pending further investigation, and said he did not wish to apply for legal aid.

He was remanded in custody and the case came up at Exeter Assizes before Mr Justice Singleton on a two-day trial beginning on 13 November. J.D. Casswell was the prosecuting counsel, and Mr John Lhind Pratt for the defence. Casswell outlined the case for the prosecution – that Emmert had deliberately shot Ridge in cold blood. Emmert said that Ridge 'had some hold' over his wife. After talking to Ridge at the hotel that evening the latter sprang at him, and he took out the revolver to frighten him, but intended to put it away again. He never lost his temper with Ridge, and if he wanted to kill him he would have had plenty of opportunity to do so before.

Examined by Mr Pratt, he said he had lain awake more nights than he had slept in prison, trying to remember what happened in the bedroom after Ridge moved towards him, evidently keen to attack him. Pratt then addressed the jury and invited them to find the accused guilty of manslaughter.

> There are some things,maybe only words, which would deprive any reasonable man
> of his self-control. The remark which Ridge made to the effect that Emmert could have
> his wife back after he had finished with her was the culminating factor that robbed the
> accused man of his self-control and the tragedy followed.

If Ridge was the first to advance and physically threaten Emmert, then it could be argued that the latter was acting in self-defence. However, the fact that he had gone to the hotel armed with a weapon, and the fact that Ridge's body bore several bullet wounds, suggested that this was not necessarily the case.

In summing up, the judge said he thought it was fair and just, while giving every consideration to the accused, to remember that the other man, about whom so much had been said, was dead and could not tell his side of the story. While their sympathy naturally and rightly went out to the man on trial, the jury had to look at the matter fairly and dispassionately.

J.D. Casswell, prosecuting counsel at the trial of Frederick Emmert.

If they came to the conclusion that the accused had obtained the revolver for the purpose of shooting Ridge if he did not leave his wife alone, and that he went to the inn to effect that purpose, that would be murder. If on the other hand they decided that Emmert had no intention of murder in his heart, but was provoked in such a way as to cause a reasonable man to lose his self-control and fire the revolver, their verdict must be one of manslaughter. He also reminded them that if a woman changed her mind and decided she preferred some other man to her lawful husband, it did not justify the husband in killing either of them. 'Remember, human life is more valuable in this country than, perhaps, in some others. It is right and proper that it should be so.'

The jury were out for an hour, before returning with a verdict of guilty, while adding a strong recommendation to mercy. The judge sentenced Emmert to death, but promised that their recommendation would be passed to the appropriate quarters. Albert Pierrepoint had arrived in the city to prepare for his duties as executioner when, two weeks later, a reprieve was issued and the sentence was commuted to life imprisonment.

27

'I SAW HER HOME'

Haldon Moor, 1949

Sidney Chamberlain was born in Newport in 1917, and moved to Devon during childhood. There was a history of epilepsy in the family, with his father being subject to seizures, which often lasted up to thirty minutes at a time. Sidney also had occasional fits, during which he would foam at the mouth. He was prone to violent behaviour, and had a tendency to attack other people with his hands for no reason, unable to remember afterwards what he had done. The most serious incident took place when he was a child of eight. He struck his sister Florence in the face with a pair of scissors, and she was left blind in the left eye.

At the age of fifteen he suffered a severe head injury and spent two weeks in hospital. When he was seventeen he was caught stealing money from a gas meter, and sent to a training school for young offenders in Exmouth, the first of several brushes with the law. During his teenage years he moved around England and Wales. Two years later, in 1936, he was sent to borstal for three years for house-breaking and stealing. He evidently served a shorter period than this, for only two years afterwards he was before the court at Glamorgan Assizes, where he received twelve months for stealing and driving away motor cars without the owners' consent. Just a year later, at Exeter, he was given another nine months in prison for stealing. This was followed by another appearance at Devon Assizes in 1940 for being armed with an offensive weapon with intent to rob, for which he served two years. By this time he had become a habitual offender, and was convicted yet again in 1942, 1943 and 1946 for such offences as store-breaking and stealing.

At some date between these misdemeanours he was married. However, by 1948 he was living at Ellis Place, Heavitree, Exeter, and having an affair with Doreen Messenger, who also lived in Heavitree, at Meadow Way. At fifteen, she was less than half his age. How much she knew of his previous history, if anything at all, is unknown. It can only be assumed that she was too trusting for her own good, and that at the same time Sidney was careful to keep the less pleasant sides of his character well hidden.

Doreen's parents, Cecil and Blanche, strongly disapproved of the liaison. They knew that he was already married, and even if he was a bachelor, the age difference between them was enough to make him quite unsuitable for their daughter, who was still only a child. It did not help their cause that, in her mother's words, Doreen was 'a big girl' who could easily have been taken for at least seventeen. Whether they were aware of his police record is another matter. Chamberlain's wife also ordered him to break off the liaison. For a while Doreen and Sidney stopped seeing each other, but later they resumed their affair and by the New Year of 1949 they were arranging regular meetings once more.

On the afternoon of 18 February, after finishing a day's work at the bookbinding department of James Townsend & Sons, a printing firm at Little Queen Street, Exeter, Doreen returned home. She had arranged to meet Sidney, and they drove to Teignmouth, where they intended to go to the cinema. When they arrived there, Doreen changed her mind, so they drove to nearby Haldon Hill and parked the car in what she referred to as their 'special place'. They talked about the problems in their relationship, he kissed her and she began to cry, saying that she would rather be dead than leave him. They stayed on the moor nearly all night, and only when dawn drew near did she realise how long they had spent together. She said she would get a good hiding from her parents when she returned home, and she did not want to go. Sidney put his hands round her neck and began to squeeze.

After some moments, her body began to shudder. He stopped the pressure on her throat and asked her if she was all right. She said nothing, but leaned forward and kissed him. He continued to squeeze her until she was unconscious. He noticed she was still breathing, so he took off his belt and strangled her with it. He then lifted her out of the car, laid her on the ground, stripped her naked and made love to her.

Meanwhile, at 2.30 a.m. on 19 February, Blanche had reported to police at Exeter that Doreen, expected home to tea the previous afternoon, was still not back. Her daughter, she said, was a quiet girl, and 'not in the habit of staying out late'. She gave them Chamberlain's name and address.

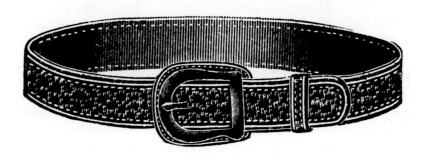

At 11.30 a.m. that day Alfred Steer, a council roadman who lived at Ideford, was cycling back from work when he noticed a bundle of clothing on the ground near a little-used track at Beggar's Bush, Ashcombe Forest. When he went to examine further, he was horrified to discover a naked corpse underneath. He immediately reported it to the police, and the body was removed to the mortuary at Torbay Hospital, Doreen's parents were informed and travelled to Torquay to give formal identification. The pathologist, Dr G. Lynch, performed a post-mortem examination and sent a report to Mr E. Hutchings, the South Devon coroner. Superintendent Stone and CID officers from Newton Abbot made a further visit to Beggar's Bush, where they spent some time examining the spot where the body was found and the surrounding area.

When detectives went to Chamberlain's address, there was no sign of him. Perhaps fortuitously, roadblocks had been set up in the area as a prisoner was on the run from Princetown Gaol. On the morning of 20 February, Chamberlain was seen driving a large saloon car. When he ignored a constable's hand signal to stop at Plymbridge, the policeman followed him on his motorcycle, until he drove the car into a side road where it struck a bank. As he emerged from the vehicle, he was arrested and taken to the police station at Plymouth. On being questioned, Chamberlain said he had taken Miss Messenger for a ride in his car and dropped her at a bus stop near her home. When the police told him that her body had been found and that she had been strangled, he answered, 'I have had nothing to do with that. I saw her home.'

Later, Chamberlain realised there was nothing to be gained in denying any knowledge of her death. He made a detailed statement, describing what had taken

Plymbridge, where Sidney Chamberlain was apprehended while trying to escape from the police.
(© Derek Tait)

place on the moor, from the time that they started talking, to her bursting into tears, his putting his hands around her throat and then leaving her body on the ground. When he lifted her from the car, he said, she was still alive, and that was when he undressed her:

> I must have laid down with her for a time. I don't know what time it was, but it started to get light. She was getting cold then because I could feel it, so I took the belt off her neck, laid her out, and covered her over. I know you found her covered over with a coat and dress on the top part and her other clothes were under her head. So I kissed her goodbye. Of course, she did not know that because she was dead.

When he was searched, a farewell note written to his sister was found in his pocket, in which he said he was going to kill himself – taking 125 aspirins 'to make sure'. Part of the note read:

> I cannot carry on like I have been doing for the last few days, so I am going to bring it to an end, because I just cannot go on without seeing Doreen. I miss her such a lot. She was very young, but I love her much more than I do my own life. I would like to see her once more before I end my own life, but I suppose that is impossible now.

On 21 February, Chamberlain was taken under police guard from Plymouth and charged with murder in an office converted into a temporary courtroom at Newton Abbot police station, and remanded in custody.

The two-day trial began on 16 June at Exeter Assizes, with Mr Justice Jones presiding, Mr Casswell and Mr Trapnell for the prosecution, Henry Elam and R. Ormrod for the defence. Chamberlain's statements and part of the letter to his sister were read out, while two policemen involved in the case took the witness stand. Inspector John Vicary of Barnstaple testified as to Chamberlain's contradictory statements regarding what happened when Miss Messenger was killed, while Detective Superintendent Harvey spoke of Chamberlain's police record and previous offences. He added that he had known the prisoner for about eight years, and had always regarded his intelligence as below average.

Dr Paul Sandifer, who had been a civilian specialist in neuro-psychiatry to the RAF, described how he had seen the prisoner twice since his arrest, and that he had been smiling as he related having had sex with Doreen's naked body after she was dead. The past events described in court were compatible with epilepsy, and suggested a form of the disease in which there was a disturbance in consciousness without seizures. Cross-examined by Mr Elam, Dr Sandifer said it would not be significant if Chamberlain had had no epileptic episodes since his arrest. Apart from the hearsay evidence, continued the doctor, there was also evidence of mental disorder covered by the term psychopath; 'he showed typical personality characteristics such as a gross deficit in the appreciation of shame, guilt, and remorse.' He was sure Chamberlain was a psychopath with a mental age of eleven or twelve.

Detail from a newspaper cutting reporting the opening of the trial of Sidney Chamberlain.
(© Steve Fielding)

SHE DIDN'T KNOW OF KISS—SHE WAS DEAD

Alleged statement

THE story of a farewell kiss was told at Devon Assizes yesterday when Sidney Archibald Frederick Chamberlain, 31, pleaded not guilty of murdering Doreen Primrose Messenger, 15, whose body was found on Haldon Moor, near Chudleigh, on February 19.

Mr. J. D. Casswell, K.C., opening the case, said the defence would be one of insanity. He said that Chamberlain made a statement that on the evening of February 18 he drove Doreen into he country as he usually did.

"We got into the back of the car and we were kissing each other. She said that rather than leave me she would rather be dead." the statement went on.

"We stayed cuddling

Doreen Messenger, the dead girl

Dr John Matheson, principal medical officer at Brixton Prison, said he had had many conversations with Chamberlain during his ten weeks in prison. At no time did he show any signs of epilepsy, and neither was there any reference to epileptic manifestations by Chamberlain in any prison record. He considered that in the light of Chamberlain's statement to the police and what he told him, he knew what he was doing on the day the girl met her death, and that what he was doing was wrong. Asked by Casswell to describe a psychopath, Dr Matheson replied:

> A psychopath is essentially a selfish man. He thinks only of himself and is usually only concerned in the immediate gratification of his desires. If prevented from satisfying those immediate desires he may get very violent.

When asked by Mr Casswell if a man in that state, a psychopath, was necessarily insane, Dr Matheson answered emphatically that he was not. When cross-examined by Mr Elan, he said he had heard evidence of suicidal tendencies shown by Chamberlain, but he attached little weight to it. He agreed that Chamberlain was a psychopath, and that it was possible for a person to be a psychopath and an epileptic at the same time.

Mr Elan invited the jury to return a verdict of guilty but insane. He pointed out that Chamberlain had laid the girl's body out, covered her over and made his escape without attempting to conceal the body. Did it strike them, he asked, that his actions were those of a normal person? Elan himself was sure that the prisoner must have been mad. As in several other murder trials at around this time, it was largely a matter of whether his actions demonstrated he was 'mad or bad'.

In summing up, the judge said that the jury would be satisfied on evidence that Chamberlain killed the girl, and that being so, they would find him guilty of murder unless they believed that when he did so he was insane. They had to ask themselves whether when he killed her, he was labouring under defective reasoning, due to a disease of the mind, and did not know the nature and quality of the act he was committing. He referred to what he called the unusual course taken by Mr Elam in asking for Chamberlain's record to be given to the court. That was to invite the jury to draw the conclusion that he was not of sound mind, but they might come to the conclusion that the record indicated he was of bad character.

While there was plainly some doubt about Chamberlain's mental condition at the time, and his responsibility for the murder, the jury were not prepared to give him the benefit of the doubt. It took them half an hour to find him guilty. He stood with his hands folded and heard the verdict apparently unmoved, slowly shaking his head as he mouthed the word 'no' when asked by the Clerk of Assize whether he had anything to say why a sentence of death should not be passed. The judge donned the

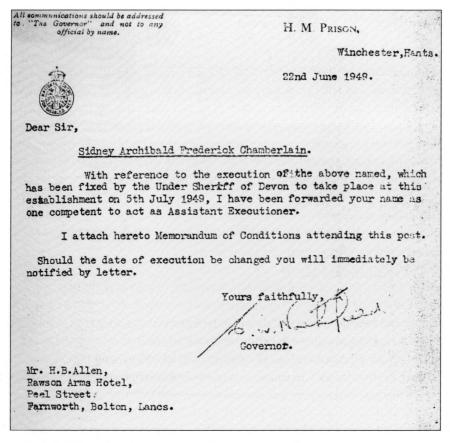

All communications should be addressed to "The Governor" and not to any official by name.

H. M. PRISON,

Winchester, Hants.

22nd June 1949.

Dear Sir,

Sidney Archibald Frederick Chamberlain.

With reference to the execution of the above named, which has been fixed by the Under Sheriff of Devon to take place at this establishment on 5th July 1949, I have been forwarded your name as one competent to act as Assistant Executioner.

I attach hereto Memorandum of Conditions attending this post.

Should the date of execution be changed you will immediately be notified by letter.

Yours faithfully,

Governor.

Mr. H.B.Allen,
Rawson Arms Hotel,
Peel Street,
Farnworth, Bolton, Lancs.

A detail of the letter from HM Prison, Winchester, to Harry Allen, assistant executioner, regarding Sidney Chamberlain's forthcoming execution. (© Steve Fielding)

Details of the assistant
hangman's diary referring
to Sidney Chamberlain's
execution. (© Steve Fielding)

Albert Pierrepoint.
(© Steve Fielding)

black cap and passed sentence of death, to be followed by silence broken only by the
sobbing of Mrs Oxenford, the condemned man's sister.

Chamberlain was executed at Winchester by Albert Pierrepoint and Harry Allen
on 28 July. In the process he became the last but one convicted murderer in Devon to
be executed.

Note: The last man was Thomas Eames, who was found guilty of murdering his
estranged wife at Plymouth in February 1952 and hanged at Bristol. (See *Devon
Murders*, Chapter 35)

28

'IF I CANNOT HAVE HER NOBODY ELSE WILL'

The offence of stalking has always been a grey area in legal terms, and there is officially no offence which is described thus in law. Attempts to rectify this anomaly in England and Wales, defined in the Stalking Bill, failed in 1996, as it was considered that the proposed offence failed to distinguish between reasonable and unreasonable conduct. The situation was rectified by the enactment of a Protection from Harassment Act, which was passed by parliament and came into force the following year. This made it a criminal offence, punishable by up to six months imprisonment, 'to pursue a course of conduct which amounts to harassment of another on two or more occasions'.

There has never been anything new about obsessive behaviour. Yet if such legislation or anything resembling it and subsequent safeguards had been in place fifty years earlier, lives would almost certainly have been saved, including that of 17-year-old Jean Agnes Burnett.

Brian Gordon Churchill was born in Cheltenham in 1932. During adolescence he moved to Exeter, and lived at Topsham Road. Towards the end of 1951 he found a job in Leonards' shoe shop in Exeter High Street, but he appeared to have problems with working alongside mostly female staff, and in March 1952 he left. His situation was doubtless exacerbated by the fact that he had become infatuated with one of his colleagues. The target of his feelings, Jean Burnett, lived with her parents at Wykes Road. Although she neither liked nor trusted Churchill, and was sensible enough not to do anything to encourage his advances, he became completely obsessed with her, and this continued after he had left the shop. It was possible that his behaviour led to a complaint to the management by Jean, or by others on her behalf, resulting in his dismissal.

Unable or unwilling to find employment elsewhere, time hung heavy on his hands, and with nothing meaningful to occupy his time, Churchill's fixation with Jean became ever more intense. Throughout this time he kept a diary, which made his intentions disturbingly clear. On 10 March, at around the time he left Leonards, he wrote:

> J. Burnett must die before I do because I was too old for her. She only laughed at me and thought me soft. I thought a lot of her once, and would have done anything for her. If I cannot have her nobody else will. One day we shall be together always.

Three weeks later, he indicated in his diary a wish to join her: 'I pray to God we could die together.'

Another entry for 17 April, after he had been following Jean at close range, made a more specific reference to his ultimate intention:

> Went to fair...saw J.B./L.S. Walked round with them. I tried her best. I shall never forget tonight, but I shall kill her one day soon.

L.S. was probably Lorna Stevens, who was one of Jean's best friends and a fellow worker in the shoe shop. By this time, Churchill was regularly following Jean, stalking her and keeping an eye on her movements. On 18 June, he recorded that he saw her waiting for a bus, and he 'felt more for her than ever before.' Four days later, he wrote, 'I going [sic] to hang soon. This year it has dwelt on my mind more than any day. The next time I see her, I am ready.'

The obsession was growing stronger day by day, and on 6 July he noted, 'Dreamt of J.B. again. This I cannot stand much longer...will kill her next week. Will be prepared. I go mad when I see her. Will be ended soon next time.' Twelve days later, on 18 July, he wrote: 'Most likely the last time I will enter in this diary the way I feel to kill.'

On 22 July, Jean caught the morning bus to work in Exeter High Street as normal, and Churchill followed her as she got on the vehicle. When she left her seat on the top deck to get off, Churchill leapt up, seized hold of her and plunged a 12-inch curved Oriental dagger into her stomach, penetrating her liver. He then ran from the scene, leaving the driver and other passengers to deal with his barely conscious and profusely bleeding victim. Jean was taken to the Royal Devon and Exeter Hospital, where doctors hoped she would recover. However the wound was too deep, and despite emergency surgery, she died that afternoon.

Running away down a busy street during the rush hour after such an incident was a forlorn hope, and Churchill was immediately apprehended by police in Topsham Road. At the police station he initially gave his name as Hancock, and he was remanded for attempted murder. When told Miss Burnett was still alive, he muttered that 'she ought to be dead by now'. When news of the girl's death reached the police, the charge became one of murder and he was remanded in custody.

Two views of Exeter High Street.

The trial opened on 30 October in Exeter Guildhall under Mr Justice Devlin, with John Maude prosecuting and Mr J. Scott-Henderson defending.

It was revealed that Churchill had been accompanied by his solicitor and three warders to a wood near Digby Hospital, where he uncovered a sodden diary from under a pile of leaves. Extracts of the diary were read out in court. On one page in the diary was a list of murderers, arranged by method and according to whether the victims were male or female.

Scott-Henderson made a strong case for Churchill's insanity at the time of the murder, and he called several witnesses to support this assertion. His probation officer told the court that Churchill had been under his supervision after he had narrowly avoided drowning in a boat with three other boys in the Channel. He had become very bitter after losing his job at Leonards, and the probation officer advised him to see a doctor, as he appeared to be heading for a nervous breakdown. The defence coss-examined witnesses who described Churchill's upbringing as 'terrible'.

The jury was asked by Mr J. Scott-Henderson to consider that although Churchill was at present a sane man, he was insane at the time of the stabbing:

Can you imagine a sane man planning to commit murder outside the Guildhall on a busy morning on top of a bus and having in his possession the recorded intention in an Army pay-book he had formed to carry out his deed? I submit that the two diaries and the circumstances in which they came to be made and found are the strongest indication of insanity.

Mr Maude disagreed. 'It shows this man was obsessed with the idea of murdering somebody. A careful examination of the diary is extremely revealing.' He re-read selected extracts from the diary, adding afterwards:

It is quite, quite clear this man knew perfectly well he was going to kill the girl, understood it was wrong, and expected to get hanged for it. This diary was buried – and no wonder. On one of these pages he has got a list of persons who murdered other people. It relates generally to the method and whether it was a man or a woman. It is quite obvious week after week this young man was knowing full well that if he did this killing he was likely to be hanged. He mentioned the fact. He expected to be hanged. He was determined to do it. He did do it.

When it was put to him that Churchill was 'a peculiar and unusual type' and that he had the desire to kill the girl for the obvious motive of jealousy, Maude continued, 'Everyone agrees that he is not insane as he sits there. He has been sitting there during this trial a perfectly sane man, though he is without doubt unusual.'

In summing up, the judge said that the question the jury had to decide was whether Churchill was legally responsible for his actions or not. The consideration of questions of mitigation was not for the jury, but was the responsibility of other persons. It was for the jury to decide whether he was legally responsible, but not the degree to which he was responsible. The rule of law which defined whether a man was or was not responsible for his act was over a century old:

It may be said, and it was said, I think, by one of the doctors for the defence that the law has in effect lagged far behind medical science and knowledge of the mind. There can be no doubt that medical science has made vast strides since then in the knowledge and workings of a man's mind, and all sorts of matters being done a hundred years ago, perhaps, of wickedness and deliberate evil are explained by those who study the workings of the mind as being things, partly at any rate, beyond his control. But it seems to me that however medical science may progress and how much further it progresses, the question a jury will decide will always be the same – did he know what he was doing?

The jury retired for forty minutes before returning with a verdict of guilty, and made no recommendation to mercy. Mr Justice Devlin sentenced Churchill to death. It would be the last time that such a sentence was ever passed in Devon.

By this time there had long been an ever-growing groundswell in legal circles against capital punishment, and any case in which there were what might be considered extenuating circumstances was scrutinised very carefully at the highest levels in the land. Although the diary that Churchill kept and eventually buried was seen as ample evidence of premeditated killing, the view that his obsessive behaviour suggested severe mental illness prevailed. On 17 November, it was announced that he had been reprieved by the Home Secretary and sentenced to life imprisonment.

Five and a half years later, there was a tragic family postscript to the episode. On 7 June 1958, it was reported in *The Times* that the partly decomposed body of Brian Churchill's mother, Winifred, had been found at their house in Tivoli Terrace, Cheltenham. The police forced an entry and her husband was escorted from the premises. Officers later waited beside his bed at Cheltenham General Hospital, where he was suffering from an injury. Research has so far failed to find what was the outcome.

29

DEATH ON VALENTINE'S DAY

Horrabridge, 1959

In 1948 Frank and Winifred Matthews were married. He was aged 34, while she was ten years older. Eight years later Mr Matthews, an excavator driver, left his wife and went to live with his brother William and sister-in-law Sylvia at The Green, Horrabridge, near Yelverton. His wife, who received 65s a week from her estranged husband by the terms of a court order, moved into a cottage on her own at Colebrook, Plympton. William Matthews was seriously ill and died in November 1956. Frank continued to live with Sylvia, until January 1959, when she decided that she wanted to go and live with relatives elsewhere, so he went to stay with his sister and brother-in-law, Mr and Mrs Horton, at Lutton.

Throughout this time Frank and Winifred had continued to see each other. Early in February 1959 they decided to try and live together again, and considered buying a house in Plymouth. On 14 February he visited her at Colebrook to discuss the matter, and suggested staying with her overnight. First of all, though, he needed to give Mr Horton and his son a lift to Plymouth, where they wanted to go shopping, and then fetch some of his belongings from Sylvia's house at Horrabridge. Winifred asked if he could give her a lift as she wanted to keep an eye on her brother-in-law, who also lived in Horrabridge, and who was unwell.

Later that day, according to Frank, they made their way back from Lutton shortly after seven o'clock that evening. While they were on the road from Walkhampton to Horrabridge, Winifred dropped something in the car from her handbag. She bent down to pick it up, and the next thing he heard was a scream. He looked round to see her legs disappearing outside the door of the vehicle. He stopped the car and got out, heard a 'funny choking noise', and realised she was badly hurt. When he tried to get her into the car to drive her to hospital, things 'seemed to go faint', and he did not know what happened next. He had 'a funny sensation', as if the road and hedge were going away from him and 'moving towards Walkhampton'. When everything

*Frank Matthews' car.
(© Assistant Chief Constable
Brian Phillips (Retd))*

*The road from Walkhampton
to Horrabridge, where
Winifred Matthews was
murdered. (© Assistant Chief
Constable Brian Phillips
(Retd))*

became normal again, he found the car was running down the hill. As he stopped it, he saw the lights of another car approaching, and he signalled to it with his torch to stop.

Mr and Mrs Scutt, from Dousland, had been driving along the road when they noticed something large in front of them. Getting out to investigate, they realised with horror that it was a human body. Nearby they saw Matthews beside his vehicle, trying to alert them, apparently distraught and begging for help. He explained that the body was that of his wife, who had fallen out of his car. The rear wheel had gone over her, and please could they help him summon an ambulance or a doctor as soon as possible. The Scuts continued their journey to Horrabridge, where they phoned the police.

Two officers arrived at the scene within minutes. One, Constable Brian Phillips, had summoned an ambulance and a doctor, who, on arrival, pronounced the woman dead. Matthews told them he had been negotiating a bend in the road when Winifred dropped some articles from her handbag. While she was trying to pick them up off the floor of the vehicle, she must have pressed on the handle, as the door flew open and she was thrown out of the car. He immediately braked as hard as he could and stopped on the offside, a short distance in front of her. The vehicle, he explained, always tended to veer to the right when he applied the brakes. It appeared to have been a tragic accident.

Constable Phillips accompanied Mr Matthews to his sister-in-law's house in Horrabridge, where he was going to spend the night. The first thing Matthews did was to reach across and fasten a bolt on the passenger door. When he was asked whether the bolt was in place when his wife was seated there, he said he had forgotten to fasten it. During the journey, and despite it being a dark winter night, Phillips had noticed minute specks on the interior of the windscreen of the car. When he took a closer look with his torch, he realised that they were small spots of blood. Matthews confirmed this by saying that he had taken a cloth from above the screen to support his wife's head, and that he had blood on his hands from her body, which must have dripped inside the car. She had severe head injuries and was covered in blood.

When asked by a CID colleague during a telephone call if he was satisfied that it had been a straightforward road accident, Phillips said that he felt there was something rather unconvincing about Mr Matthews' explanation.

That evening Matthews was given a sedative from the doctor before going to bed. Constable Phillips and the doctor were joined by Sergeant Lee at Horrabridge and

Horrabridge, c. 1915.

they examined the interior of the car, which was parked in the road about 50 feet from the house. They discovered more bloodstains and smears of blood which had run down the woodwork below the passenger door window. Then Matthews arrived, carrying a glass container, and was very surprised to see them. He explained that he had come outside to get some paraffin for lighting the fire in the morning. The policemen suspected he had intended to use it to clean off the bloodstains before anybody had noticed, in which case he was too late.

It increased their suspicion that there were grounds for further investigation, and they went to where the incident had occurred to examine the road by torchlight. What they found led them to believe that Matthews' description of events had hardly been truthful. Phillips had previously marked with chalk the position of the car and the body when he arrived on the scene. There were bloodstains on the road and fresh oil drips where the car had been. Further examination revealed blood and oil on the road at a point further back from where the body had lain, which suggested the car had stopped there before Winifred died. They decided to return in daylight and investigate more thoroughly.

CID officers then took over the investigation. The mortuary had been instructed to leave Mrs Matthews's body clothed and undisturbed for the post-mortem examination. Dr Stewart Smith, pathologist for the Exeter area, examined the body and visited the scene of the tragedy. He concluded that death was due to multiple head injuries, and found a depression in the head consistent with being run over by the wheel of a car. There were other, smaller injuries to the head, sufficient to cause a fracture of the skull. In his opinion, these were inflicted by a blunt instrument from the toolbox behind the driver's seat. This contained several hammers, one of which had traces of blood on the handle. There were also smudges of clay and particles of shale on the dead woman's clothing, which could not have come from the tarmac road. The torso did not contain abrasive injuries of the type normally associated with somebody coming into contact with a tarmac road. Detectives found a swathe of disturbed material, mostly clay and shale, some distance back from where the body had been. It suggested that Mrs Matthews had been thrown across a grass verge and down a rough bank leading to common ground, and had been dragged feet first up the bank and laid in the road. Bloodstained stones were discovered at various distances from the bottom of the bank; a knitted glove lay nearby, matching the one found on the body, and a small thorn bush with splashes of blood on it. The bush was taken up and later exhibited in court together with the stones. It was now apparent that the police had a murder case on their hands.

Motor Patrol Constable Burgess examined the car and tested the brakes. He found that the car veered to the left and not to the right, as Matthews had claimed. A practical test by an assistant groping on the floor for articles failed to open the passenger door, even after heavy pressure was applied. There was a layer of undisturbed mud adhering to the underside of the chassis, which led to the conclusion that at no stage had a body been dragged underneath the car and run over by the rear wheel.

On 20 February, Matthews was interviewed by police in the presence of his solicitor in Plymouth. He continued to insist that his wife had fallen out of the car, and a rear wheel had gone over her head. The blood spots on the seat, frame of the windscreen and glove compartment could be explained by his having picked up her hat and put it under her head, which was covered in blood. He went back to the car to get some rags, which he kept above the windscreen, and put those under her head as well to try and make her more comfortable.

Dr Charles Hunt, a pathologist based at the South-Western Forensic Laboratory in Bristol, and an assistant were asked to examine the vehicle and the ground where the incident occurred. They showed that all bloodstains on the road, in the area around the thorn bush, on the bush as well as in the vehicle, were all from blood group B, the same group as Mrs Matthews. Several strands of human hair were found on the car door, rear tyre, thorn bush, and several stones nearby, as well as fibres from her clothing. There was no blood or hair found under the vehicle consistent with an accidental fall from inside.

The suspect's clothing was taken for examination, and further incriminating evidence came to light. His shoes had just been cleaned when they were taken from him, and he had washed the overalls he had worn, leaving them drying over the fire. Blood belonging to the same blood group was found on other items of clothing and his shoes had traces of blood, clay and shale in the soles.

Matthews could not account for any of the inconsistencies in his story, but stood by everything he had previously said. He appeared in court at Tavistock on 21 April, formally charged with the wilful murder of his wife. David Johnson, acting on his behalf, said he would plead not guilty.

For the prosecution, Peter Barnes alleged that Matthews had driven his wife to a spot on the road, stopped his car where the first oil stains marked the road, then battered her over the head with a blunt instrument – probably a hammer from the toolbox – where she sat in the passenger seat. She managed to get out and tried to run for her life, but her husband pursued her and caught up with her as she stumbled, either over rocks or a thorn bush. He struck her again, probably with the bloodstained stones which had been found scattered nearby, until she was unconscious, and dragged her up the bank on to the road, where he reversed the wheel over her head, which accounted for the depression in her skull. He then parked his vehicle on the offside of the road further along to give the impression that she had fallen out and landed where she was lying. In Barnes's view, it was 'as callous and brutal a murder as could possibly be imagined.'

Detective Sergeant C.J. Tarr, who led the investigation, reported that he had driven at 30mph along the two routes Matthews could have taken from Lutton, where he had called with his wife in the car to collect some belongings from his sister's house and left just before 7 p.m.. It would have left Matthews an uninterrupted half an hour to kill his wife and stage the so-called accident.

Evidence was also given by Mr Scutt, whom Matthews had flagged down after the incident, and Ivor and Patricia Trembath of Walkhampton. They had been walking along the road and also saw the body of Winifred Matthews lying on the road.

Matthews was sent for trial at Exeter Assizes, where he pleaded not guilty to murder. Proceedings began on 19 June under Mr Justice Donovan, with Mr J.T. Moloney for the prosecution and Mr Norman Skelhorn QC for the defence, and lasted four and a half days.

Among the witnesses called was Thomas Passmore, a motor engineer who worked at Plymouth. He had examined the car and carried out road tests, during which he discovered that the passenger door had been thrown violently open, and a mark made on the vehicle towards the rear where contact had been made. The passenger seat was also found to be very badly secured. All this reduced the likelihood of the death having been accidental.

Dr Smith was questioned about the wounds on Patricia Matthews's body, and conceded that in his view one of these could have been caused by her falling on to the road. Nevertheless other, less severe wounds might well have been caused by her being thrown over a steep bank, or by being deliberately hit with stones. One of the blows had possibly been made by a blunt instrument without a cutting edge, possibly something like the flat side of a tyre lever.

Dr Hunt had been present at the examination of Winifred's body at Plymouth mortuary on 10 June. Seven wounds to the head were discernible, but the eighth was no longer clearly visible because of decomposition. He said that the fractures in the skull might have been caused by the same injury, a severe blow or crushing by a heavy weight, such as being run over by a heavy wheel, and four of the wounds had probably been inflicted by a blunt instrument with at least one straight edge, such as a tyre lever or heavy spanner. They were not the sort of injuries consistent with having fallen from a car.

William Gliddon, a staff biologist from the forensic laboratory at Bristol, testified to having found hairs from a human head at the base of the bush exhibited in court, as well as wool fibres caught on twigs, similar to those of the black cardigan Winifred had been wearing. There were spots of blood on the bush, and on the stones, which looked as if they had been deliberately scattered in an effort to avoid detection.

In summing up for the prosecution, Sumner submitted that the murder may not have been planned, but more probably followed a sudden argument. This did not alter the fact that what had happened was no accident, and in particular the number of wounds on the victim's head made it clear that she had been deliberately killed.

For the defence, Skelhorn contended that rational motive was lacking. If it was suggested that Matthews killed his wife because he was separated from her and paying her under the terms of the court order, and because he was not making the payments regularly, was that a genuine reason for murder?

Whether he meant to kill her or lost his temper was open to doubt. Nevertheless, the jury only took forty-five minutes to decide that it was murder with malice aforethought. Telling Matthews that they 'have seen through your cunning', the judge sentenced him to life imprisonment.

After the sentence was read out, the judge recommended that all the police officers involved in the case should be commended for their efforts. In an official letter, the Director of Public Prosecutions made special mention of Constable Phillips, 'whose powers of observation when originally called to the scene ensured that the case was treated as one of suspected murder within a very short time of its commission.' Phillips later rose to become Assistant Chief Constable of Devon and Cornwall Constabulary. Had he not noticed the small spots of blood on a dark February night, and had he accepted Mr Matthews's explanation at face value, Winifred's death would almost certainly have been treated as a tragic accident.

BIBLIOGRAPHY

BOOKS

Chard, Judy, *Devon Tales of Mystery and Murder,* Newbury: Countryside, 2001
— *Murder and Mystery in Devon.* Chudleigh: Orchard Publications, 1994
Eddleston, John J., *The Encyclopedia of Executions,* London: John Blake, 2004
Fielding, Steve, *Hanged at Winchester,* Stroud: The History Press, 2010
— *The Hangman's Record, Vol. 1, 1868-1899; Vol. 2, 1900-1929; Vol. 3, 1930-1964,* Beckenham: CBD, 1994-2005
Harrison, John Grant, *The Penalty was Death: Nineteenth-century crime and executions in Devon,* Tiverton: Halsgrove, 1997
James, Trevor, *Bodies on the Moor,* Chudleigh: Orchard, 2004
Oxford Dictionary of National Biography (also available online)
Sly, Nicola, *A Ghostly Almanac of Devon and Cornwall,* Stroud: The History Press, 2009
— *Murder by Poison: A Casebook of British Historic Murders,* Stroud: The History Press, 2009

NEWSPAPERS AND WEBSITES

Birmingham Daily Post
Cheshire Observer
Illustrated Police News
Morning Chronicle
Penny Illustrated Paper
Reynolds's Newspaper
The Standard
The Times
Trewman's Exeter Flying Post
Western Morning News

Exeter memories website: www.exetermemories.co.uk

INDEX